Language
Programs
in the
Public
Schools

Edited by Jewell A. Friend

Southern Illinois University Press

Carbondale and Edwardsville

Feffer & Simons, Inc.

London and Amsterdam

Library of Congress Cataloging in Publication Data
Main entry under title:

Language programs in the public schools.

Includes index.
1. English language—Study and teaching (Secondary)
2. English language—Grammar. I. Friend, Jewell A.
LB1631.L25   428'.007'12   76−58879
ISBN 0−8093−0794−4
ISBN 0−8093−0811−8 pbk.

Contents

Language Programs in the Public Schools

1 General Introduction

Jewell A. Friend

RATIONALE

If, as few will deny, language is our primary means of shaping reality as human beings; if, as human beings, men are constantly immersed in some kind of language experience; if the intensity and richness of that language experience sharpen insights; if insights are directly related to the formation of attitudes and values, then it should follow that the student who develops the greatest sensitivities to the nuances of and the power implicit in language would be the "most" human, the most insightful, the most reliable in terms of attitudes and values. Yet, the language experience of the English student is probably the most rigid, restrictive, prescriptive, unrealistic, alienating of all. This book considers the reasons for the omission or irrelevance of the language experience in many English classrooms, the resources available that suggest change, and the liberal rewards we might justifiably anticipate.

REASONS

The English teacher is a "thing apart." She is distinguished from the remainder of society by a verbal stamp that often takes the

1

form of a whispered admonition behind a cupped hand: "Watch your language. She's an English teacher." In circumstances marked by greater candor the pigeonholing is implicit in apologies or confessions such as, "I just loved *Silas Marner*, and I cried when I read *Wuthering Heights*, but the reason why I didn't take more English . . . I mean the reason *that* I didn't take more English was because . . . I mean *was that* . . ." Occasionally, "O, you must know Mrs. Hoeffling. She's the teacher *who* I learned all my grammar from . . . I mean *from whom* . . . I never could get that straight." The full reality of the occupational stamp comes with "Can I . . . I mean, uh . . . May I kiss you good-night?"

The fact is, however, that a good many English teachers enjoy and encourage this dubious prestige. They feel superior, above the world of slang, scatology, teen-age jargon, linguistic liberality. Many other teachers, fainthearted or wearied by the rites, avoid identifying themselves with *English* teaching specifically. English teaching in a science-oriented society is an equivocal advantage. At any rate, the isolation is manifest in every aspect of social intercourse from the golf links to the dinner party to the faculty lounge to the dentist's office to the automobile repair shop. A friend of mine reported calling in a local plumber to correct a problem in the bathroom. The plumber was an elderly gent with a fine South Midland dialect who had lived through the labor struggles in an area called "Bloody Herrin," a local mining town. My friend, standing in the doorway of the room, listened with awe to the history of the labor movement of the thirties—with all the charm and embellishments of the local dialect. Then, the phone rang and my friend stepped into another room, picked up the telephone, and after a brief interval said, "Yes, this is he." When he finished the conversation, he returned to the bathroom to chat further with the plumber. The old gent asked, "What did you say you teach?" My friend hadn't said, but now he answered, "English." "Yup, I thought so," the plumber mumbled. They didn't exchange another word despite my friend's repeated overtures.

Isolated in a world where economic and political values supersede humanistic values, English teachers whose *raison d' être* has theoretically, at least, been humanistic, often become defensive and disinclined to work within a nonscientific framework. They write strictly behavioral objectives, select content and plan sequential lockstep experiences in language, and evaluate student growth in terms of pre- and post-tests (objective, of course) in factors of one hundred. This kind of formulaic procedure facilitates grading (always of the *student*; rarely of the teacher, the methods, the materials, etc.), progress reports, and all kinds of accountability credentials. What aspect of language activity fits most readily and most comfortably into such a plan? Schoolroom grammar, of course. "It was good enough for my father and for me and it is good enough for my sons! It worked for us; it will work for him, too." The fact is that such practices did not work! What we have as a result of schoolroom grammar drills is a mass of linguistically provincial noncommunicants.

Isn't it strange that the essence of the isolation English teachers suffer is traceable to such schoolroom experiences? Isn't it strange also that in a nonhumanistic adult world—the world which isolates the English teacher, the world toward which young people express such hostility—isn't it strange that more English teachers don't turn toward the domain of youth where the demand for humanism, idealism, and honest examination of values is so great? Wouldn't the English teacher's answering the youthful cry for relevant, intense, aesthetic experiences in the classroom enjoin much of the prevalent discord and enhance opportunities for social understanding and human harmony? And, wouldn't an examination of language as an index to humane values and as a vehicle for social expression be appropriate?

Another factor inhibiting the development of relevant language experience programs for the student is the narrow definition of *language*. This is traceable to the inadequacy of English education of teachers, administrators, and parents. An administrator once said, "I can tell from your speech that you come from New York; so, don't tell me what ought to be taught in English classes. I know." His field had not been English, but someplace he had learned 1) that terminal *r*'s are not pronounced by New Yorkers and 2) that such a dialectal peculiarity marked an individual as potentially aggressive, threatening, or uncooperative. This kind of dialectal prejudice permeates the home and school environments of too many students. It is the sad result of highly prescriptive and narrow indoctrination in the nature and use of language.

Although educators will agree in principle that people learn at different rates and through different experiences, their English language classrooms are often characterized by invalid premises, outdated materials and inflexible methods. Unless language experiences can be measured, described in detail beforehand, shown to fit a specific course outline or to lead to a written composition, they are often unacceptable. If the student (whom we acknowledge learns in his own way and at his own pace) is allowed to become the center of the language experience, then uniformity must be sacrificed, tests of verbal maturity will have limited value, computers and computerized school personnel would have to be reprogrammed.

Let's consider for a moment a few instances of invalid premises, outdated materials, and inflexible methods. For more than a century now the study of language has been regarded in many schools as the study of grammar exclusively—not grammar in the linguists' sense, but grammar as verbal etiquette. If this definition has not applied in theory (that is, in statements of philosophy prepared for perusal by administrators or regional accreditation teams), it has in practice. One of the most commonly used texts is a schoolroom grammar written and published over twenty-five years ago. For a quarter of a century students using this text have gone through drills on the use of shall-will, who-whom, etc., despite the fact that their own usage and that of all of those to whom they are exposed contradict the rules prescribed and implicit in the drill. Such approaches to grammar as this, such comfortable linguistic certainties with all their moral overtones may soothe the troubled brow of English teachers and administrators unaware of the events of the last twenty-five years—three wars with all the lexical and intercultural influences on language; space exploration with its

Language Programs

new lexicon and incumbent semantic shifts; forging of new frontiers in mass media with resultant divided usages and linguistic sophistication; innumerable developments in linguistic science with various methods of grammatical analysis and insights into the psycholinguistic processes—but they are of little comfort, interest, or relevance to the student who sees a life beyond the school walls.

A second premise that has contributed to the undue prestige of the schoolroom grammar is its identification with traditional classical grammars of such scholars as Otto Jespersen, Henry Sweet, and George Curme. A few of the more obvious distinctions between classical traditional and the traditional schoolroom grammars may suffice to refute this premise.

a) The classical traditional approach to grammatical analysis bases its analysis on the written language but acknowledges distinctions between written and oral forms. The traditional schoolroom grammar avoids distinctions between written and oral forms.

b) The classical traditional grammars make the distinction between tense and aspect. The schoolroom grammars make no such distinctions clear, but mislead the student with terms such as "perfect tenses" or "progressive tenses."

c) Classical traditional grammars treat case as a morphological entity and so simplify case for nouns into common or genitive. Schoolroom grammars assign nouns arbitrarily in terms of function, without regard to form.

d) Classical traditional grammars distinguish between lexical and grammatical meaning, a task the schoolroom grammar ignores despite the fact that any understanding of how a language system works demands such considerations.

e) The classical traditional grammarian is quick to acknowledge limitations of his descriptive method and to cite alternate approaches. Schoolroom grammars make arbitrary decisions, failing to cite alternatives.

f) Classical traditional grammars distinguish between various kinds of genitives (possession, origin, description, character, material, partitive, etc.) and the forms they may take (inflectional, periphrastic, adjunctive). Schoolroom grammars make no such distinctions, generally use *genitive* and *possessive* synonymously, and often confine formal treatment to the inflection.

g) Classical grammars acknowledge linguistic flux as a natural phenomenon. Schoolroom grammars ignore such change manifest in divided usage, semantic shift, co-occurrence constraints, etc.

In brief, the scientific invalidity of schoolroom grammars is not the primary concern at this writing; however, what is is the misinformation conveyed through innocence or ignorance of English language teachers, their colleagues, and the community that supports the school system.

A third premise which misleads those responsible for providing meaningful language experiences for the student is the notion that ideas and practices that have met with approval in the past and so are stamped "traditional" are somehow sacrosanct. The schoolroom grammar approach, the drill approach, the mental discipline approach, the prestige-usage approach all become a litany of Thou Shalts without which Thou Shalt Not Work As A Telephone Operator for General Electric.

Most students have been handling language competently and have been using it to shape their own concepts of reality since crib days. (Even in the holophrastic stages of language acquisition, the infant posits predications although his language system is different from that of adults. He does, however, have a system as psycholinguistic investigations have revealed.) Most students want to use their creative intellects and learn how to explore the world they live in; most students will resist our shaping a synthetic "reality" for them through drills and other tactics in the name of mental discipline; most students cry out for richer and more intense experiences than grammar drills provide; most students will drop out of programs before they will endure the intellectual molestation that left their parents whispering behind their cupped hands: "Watch your language. She's an English teacher."

None of the above is to deny value to the study of linguistics, theoretical or applied. It is, however, to suggest that a public high school or junior high school—where the emotional and intellectual

Language Programs

needs of students are so great, where the interests and abilities are so varied, where the walls are about to burst with unused energy —is no place for intensive grammatical drills; syntactic analysis; formulaic, lockstep catechistic adherence to linguistic absolutes of some sort or other. Language is systematic, but the nature of that system has been a matter of controversy since the days of Aristotle. That system is not so trivial a matter as can be played with or taken lightly by the disinterested, the uninterested, or the inadequately prepared. Among the many insights modern linguistics has provided are that, though systematic, language is dynamic and that all grammars "leak." Until we know a great deal more about the system underlying our language, we ought not pretend to have all the answers. Perhaps the best we can do is to pique the interest of young people who might recognize the power, the flexibility, the variety, the degrees of appropriateness of language—the servant, not the master, of man. Some may even choose to make the study of linguistics their career and hopefully throw some greater ray of light on it.

ALTERNATIVES AND RESOURCES

The premises cited at the beginning of this statement may be summarized as follows: a) language is the primary means of shaping one's perception of reality; b) humans are constantly immersed in some kind of language experience; c) insights may be sharpened in proportion to the intensity and richness of language experiences; d) insights are related to the formation of attitudes and values.

In chapter 11 of *Client-Centered Therapy* (Boston: Houghton Mifflin, 1951), Carl Rogers advances some basic propositions regarding the responses of humans to phenomena about them. He suggests that every individual exists in a continually changing world of which he himself is the center, the interpreter, the evaluator (in terms of his own perceptions, values, needs, and attitudes), the responder. What seems *real* then depends largely upon the individual's perception of phenomena, and thus there are a finite number of realities corresponding only to the number of experiencing individuals. In brief, the nature of reality depends upon how an experience serves to extend the "self." Unless there is an internal frame of reference, the individual can in no way respond meaningfully to an experience, give it value, or manifest growth from that experience. Stewart W. Holmes in *Meaning in Language* (Harcourt, 1972) goes so far as to view language as "stored experience" because of the semantic import individuals attribute to words and phrases and their visceral responses to language, nonverbal and verbal.

To see language as an index to reality, to view it as an extension of self, to recognize it as a tool for fulfilling individual needs in a world of the adolescent should be among the major objectives in English classrooms. This is in no way to deprecate the aesthetic value of language in favor of the pragmatic. When we impose our own aesthetic criteria in an English classroom, however, we rob the student of his right to respond individually to a language experience. "No spring nor summer beauty hath such grace/As I have seen in one autumnal face" may be aesthetically pleasing to an English teacher, especially those of us on the autumnal side of forty, but to insist that an eighth- or tenth- or twelfth-grader acknowledge either the beauty or the truth of Donne's lines is to challenge the student's concept of reality or to prostitute him intellectually.

A few generalizations about the adolescent's view of the real world may be pertinent. He is often highly moralistic, his use of scatology notwithstanding. The immoral value teachers attribute to scatological expressions may not be a part of their students' own value system. Indeed, both the value and the meaning of terms used by adolescents are often considerably different from those of adults. To the adolescent, acts are immoral or moral; language is amoral. Second, he places high value on candor and honesty; he scorns hypocrisy. This may account for his disinclination to accept euphemisms that his elders find such comfortable cloaks for irreverence, bias, and emotional and social subterfuge. Third, he is interested in exploring and expanding his own range and depth of experience. His questions tend away from WHAT and WHEN toward HOW and WHY. *How* can I find out X? *How* can I qualify for a summer job? *How* can I become a Y? *Why* do some people do Z? *Why* can't adults recognize my need for privacy? *Why* do I have to take four years of English? Morris Sanders (*Classroom Questions*) suggests that phrasing questions in terms of HOW and WHY is one of the most effective ways of stimulating sound intellectual activities in the adolescent.

How can we make the language experience in the English classroom consistent with the adolescent's concept of reality, relevant to his needs and interests, and valid as a part of the discipline? What are the resources at our disposal? This book proposes some under units entitled "General Pedagogy," "The English Language," "Lexicography," "American English Usage," "Dialectology," "Grammar," and "Semantics."

Clearly, no book with this range can do more than provide a rationale for types of language experiences in English classrooms, explain briefly a few of the major principles and premises, and suggest a few exercises that may prove helpful to the teacher whose time for planning is limited. The book is designed to provide assistance; it is in no way meant to be a substitute for teacher education in language or linguistics. It should, however, summarize in a convenient way the theoretical and practical facets of English-language teaching that have emerged from extensive research in the area. All exercises will not be suitable to all levels or all groups of students; selectivity and modification will be an important part of the teacher's function as she works with this book.

2 General Pedagogy

J. N. Hook

HOW SHOULD THE ENGLISH
LANGUAGE BE TAUGHT?

Once, not long ago in fact, teaching the English language meant teaching only two things, grammar and usage, and those two were usually confused enough in teachers' minds that they were run together under the single rubric "grammar." Teachers taught this "grammar" in two basic ways. One way was to ask students to analyze or partially analyze sentence after sentence, picking out and labeling subjects, predicates, direct and indirect objects, personal pronouns, transitive verbs, predicate adjectives, and so on. The other way was to ask students to determine which of two usages—say *he* or *him, was* or *were*—was "correct." Day after day these two procedures were continued—for about half the total time spent in English class, according to a study made in Illinois in the 1940s by the late John J. DeBoer.

We know now that such instruction was thin, poverty-stricken, badly motivated, and on the whole unsatisfactory in its results. As this book shows, today's teachers believe that study of the English language should be rich and varied. The goals are no longer just the ability to apply grammatical labels and to determine "correctness"—the quotation marks signifying that teachers now know that customs in usage change, that ideas of correctness are somewhat fluid, that for instance *you was* and *most unkindest* and double negatives and countless other expressions were once standard and are now frowned upon, and that many of today's "correct" usages will no doubt be "wrong" in the future.

We still do need to teach grammar, but our purpose now is less to pin on labels than to build an understanding of how the English sentence works. And we do still need to teach usage, but today we do so in clear recognition of the fact that usage does change, that there is nothing eternally "right" or "wrong" about any locution, and that in teaching usage we are really giving instruction in a form of etiquette—the linguistic behavior that happens to be socially approved in the last quarter of the twentieth century.

We don't spend as much time on grammar and usage as we once did; but, if we are wise, we use the saved time on other facets of the language, discussed in some detail in other chapters of this book. Specifically, we 1) teach dialects, building an understanding that it is natural and normal for people to speak differently from one another, and building enjoyment of the diversity; 2) teach history of the language, adding depth to our students' understanding of their language and its functioning, showing how English has been enriched by contributions from around the world, and revealing the reasons for the changes that any living language constantly undergoes; 3) teach semantics, showing how people give meanings to words and how one's choices of words can influence the thinking, the emotions, and the actions of those who hear or read them; and 4) teach lexicography, showing how dictionaries may be used most intelligently by those who know how dictionaries are made.

Guidelines for the attainment of those four purposes, plus those already implied for grammar and usage, are central to this book. Some specific suggestions for attainment are offered in each chapter. In this one, stressing pedagogy, the attempt will be to isolate and illustrate a few basic principles.

THE NEED FOR AN OVERALL PLAN

There is some evidence that many teachers today are more spontaneous than they once were, that they improvise more and often let student wishes or mere chance determine content, and that detailed curriculum planning is less in vogue than it was a decade or so ago.

Certainly spontaneity is desirable, and certainly students should have a voice in determination of what they study. Certainly also a lockstep curriculum in which all ninth-graders, for instance, are doing the same things at the same time is undesirable.

But there are many gradations between rigidity and anarchy, between detailed planning and planlessness. Assuredly we wouldn't have put men on the moon if there hadn't been much planning, but it is equally true that if the planning had not been flexible, space engineers could not have coped with the endless unexpected developments. In teaching, too, we need a general plan, an outline showing where we want to go and approximately how we expect to get there, and then we need to be flexible in our specific procedures.

In teaching the English language, a school or a department should have a general plan to which all teachers subscribe in the main. This plan should indicate, first, what broad facets of the language ought to be covered in the grades included in the school. (This book provides a possible basis for such determination.) Secondly, the plan should show the grade level(s) or the course(s) that ought to devote specific and systematic attention to, say, history of the language.

The justification of such a plan is that it makes certain that no important phase of the language will be omitted or grossly neglected in the curriculum. But the plan does not prescribe the precise amount of time to be spent on each aspect of the language or tell the individual teacher how he or she should teach.

A good kind of plan is the one that offers during each three-year span (say in grades 4–6, again in 7–9, and once more in 10–12) a sustained period of time (one to six weeks, depending on grade level) to *each* of the six aspects of language considered in this book: grammar, usage, history of the language, dialects, semantics, and lexicography. Thus each student gets a systematic exposure to each aspect three times, on increasingly advanced levels. These sustained periods are then supplemented ad lib as occasion arises: semantic questions come up repeatedly during students' practice of composition, for instance, and bits of linguistic history enter into the reading of Chaucer, Shakespeare, Irving, Emerson, and other writers of the past.

Language study lends itself especially well to the relatively short elective courses now offered by many schools. For example, a semantics elective can deal with devices used by advertisers and politicians to gain their ends, or (nearer home) an inductive study of how students, their parents, and their teachers attempt to manipulate language to sway others. A language history elective may concentrate on changes in the language in either England or America, the differences between British and American English, or the contributions that foreign countries have made to the language. A grammar elective may be a condensed, simplified study of transformations. A usage elective may be historically based, with students looking at literary samplings from various periods and studying inductively the usage preferences of those periods. A lexicography elective could trace the history of dictionary making, with emphasis on Samuel Johnson, Noah Webster, and the turbulent reception of the latest Webster's unabridged. And a dialect elective may focus on variations in vocabulary or in pronunciation, or (if the community is appropriate) a student investigation of local dialectal characteristics. These are only a few suggestions, which are supplemented and amplified elsewhere in this book.

TAKING ADVANTAGE OF THE MOMENT

Instruction in language, as has already been implied, should not be confined to elective courses or to units planned within the framework of the school's English courses. Opportunities to discuss language are almost omnipresent. Knowledgeable teachers often pause in their intended routines to follow briefly a little bypath that students have become interested in. For example:

A student wonders aloud why some of our spellings (*psychology, pneumonia, doubt,* etc.) are so "odd." A few minutes of follow-up will answer part of his question and show something about how the language has developed.

Similarly, a student wonders about unusual plurals (*mice, deer, criteria,* etc.) or about the reason for the existence of "irregular" verbs (*know, freeze, be,* etc.). Again, there is opportunity to explore interesting facets of language history.

Students encounter references to the "democracy" of ancient Greece. How does our "democracy" differ from that? How and why do words change in meaning?

In a British story the class encounters "the government *are,*" and someone wonders whether it is a misprint. A discussion of usage emphasizes the point that since government consists of many persons, *are* is no less logical than *is,* but also reveals that logic and usage are not closely connected anyway.

"It takes too long to look up a word in the dictionary," a student complains. A ten-minute lesson, in how to find a word quickly, will be helpful to many students. (With young students, each equipped with a dictionary, a competitive game may be made of finding words quickly.)

MOTIVATION

The Encyclopedia of Education (1971, vol. 6, p. 411) says: "Since about 1950, several lines of research have shown that higher animals are prone to spend a great deal of time and energy actively seeking out stimulation, especially when they have no overridingly urgent matters like hunger or physical danger to deal with. They will eagerly approach and inspect unfamiliar features of the environment. All things being equal, they will vary the paths they take to their goals on successive occasions, preferring actions that ensure novelty and variety of stimulation. Human beings in particular find conditions of monotony or sensory restriction intolerable after a while and resort eagerly to any actions that produce changing sights and sounds."

In grammar and usage, one reason that old-fashioned emphasis on mere labeling and counting was not effective was that it led to such "conditions of monotony or sensory restriction." It's surely not very exciting to spend hour after hour on parsing sentences (or even on drawing sentence "trees"—the modern equivalent), and after one has done a dozen exercises on such old standbys as *who-whom* and *lie-lay*, they no longer possess much "novelty and variety of stimulation."

The modern view of language teaching, however, does make such variety possible. There's so much worth studying in language that a class can go on endlessly without repeating and can use all sorts of techniques.

Effective motivation consists in part of taking advantage of such riches, such variety. It consists also of starting with students' current interests and concerns and building upon them. It is often easier to motivate when students' curiosity has already been aroused than it is to create from scratch an entirely new interest, although that too can be done. Here are a few examples of motivation of some facets of language study:

A class whose students had predominately Anglo-Saxon names gained two new students, Kowalczyk and Ivanovich. On learning that those names mean "Smith" and "Johnson," the class was motivated to a week's study of onomastics—names, their origins, and their meanings. (A study of place-names can be no less interesting and rewarding. So can a study of how common American animals, birds, and flowers were named; e.g., *skunk* from an Indian language, *catbird* because it meows, *Jack-in-the-pulpit* because it resembles a little man standing in an old-fashioned, overarching pulpit.)

Differences in pronunciation and different names for the same thing are likely to exist in the same class; e.g., *creek* and *crick*, *soda pop* and *soft drink*. Students are interested in such differences and can be led from this localized interest to a broader consideration of dialects.

The yearbooks of some encyclopedias (*World Book* and *Britannica*) usually contain articles on newly coined or recently popularized words. These articles may serve as an impetus for a study of neologisms, how words enter the language, what kinds of words are coming in now, etc.

To develop interest in and information about lexicography, many schools have encouraged students to work cooperatively on the preparation of a dictionary of current teen-age slang.

Modern writers of advertising copy often use unusual or picturesque language. Students may search for examples and analyze what makes them unusual. (The *New Yorker* is a better-than-average source.)

To illustrate the importance of word order in the English sentence, a teacher got the woodworking shop to saw a number of small wooden cubes; she pasted a different word on each face —nouns on some cubes, transitive verbs on some, intransitive verbs on others, forms of *be* on some, adjectives, adverbs, etc. When students rolled cubes at random, grammatical sentences seldom resulted, but when a predetermined order was followed, the sentences were usually grammatical. (When they weren't, the reasons were sought.)

A class in the Ozarks studied survivals of Elizabethan English in the speech of the area.

Elementary school pupils prepared and presented a playlet in which words in a sentence were the "characters." They discussed and argued about their respective roles, who was most important, etc.

Using an article by Norman Stageberg (*English Journal*, May 1966, pp. 588 ff.) as a point of takeoff, a class collected or constructed and analyzed examples of syntactic ambiguity. (The practice was useful in combating some of their own ambiguities in speech and writing—e.g., "girl hunter," "blond artist's model," "Little Charm Motel," "modern language teaching," "cold morning bath," "The bouncer turned out a drunkard," "He washed the chair on the patio.")

INDUCTION

As may be inferred from some of the examples already given, inductive teaching is often superior to lecturing or requiring rote memorization. The inductive process requires moving from a group of specific cases to a generalization based on them, as a scientist does in his laboratory. The lecture method—which is obviously *not* inductive—may be suitable for use in some college courses, but with younger students the active participation required by the inductive method results in greater motivation and, as a rule, greater retention. Here are some examples:

The class makes a list of words ending in silent *e*—words like *fame, state,* and *like* to which suffixes may be added. On the basis of a large number of examples, the class draws up a rule that tells when the *e* should be dropped (e.g., *stating*) and when it should not (e.g., *statement*), and then applies the rule to still other silent-*e* words.

In a unit called "One Word Led to Another," a class started with *kilometer,* then thought of two other words based on *kilo* and *meter,* then two more based on each of these new words, and so on. Lively discussions occurred, and vocabulary enrichment was inevitable.

A class selects a few pages from a dictionary and examines the individual words to note the type of word formation in each; i.e., how did each of these words get into the language? Thus *blackberry* represents compounding; *blacken,* addition of an affix; to *blind,* functional shift; *bleed* (as a printing term), extension of meaning; *blight* (in some definitions), figurative language; *blasphemy,* borrowing from other languages; *brunch,* blending. (A word that was in the language in Anglo-Saxon times is regarded as native.)

As part of the study of grammar, instead of telling students

"English questions are constructed in such and such ways," the teacher asks each of them to find and copy several brief questions, which the class may analyze to discover the structures employed. (Other kinds of transformations and structures may be taught similarly.)

Instead of learning that "This usage is correct, or that one wrong," each student selects a different usage matter (e.g., *good-well, hopefully, -wise* as in *athletics-wise)* and for two or three days makes notes of examples that he finds in print, hears on radio or TV, or hears in conversation. He reports on his findings, and with his classmates, makes a judgment about the present reputability of the item.

Since not all students have the same problems in usage, it is wasteful of time to expose the whole class to items that only a few may need. Instead, commercially produced (often programmed) materials may be assigned or selected on an individual basis, according to each student's special needs.

LANGUAGE AS A SOCIAL TOOL

Excessive emphasis on grammatical analysis makes language seem rather cold and mechanical. This statement is true whether one thinks of old-fashioned parsing and sentence diagramming or new-fangled application of phrase structure rules and drawing of sentence trees. We shouldn't throw out scientific analysis entirely, but we shouldn't overdo it.

Also, excessive attention to usage fails to illuminate the humanness of language. Since the eighteenth century teachers and books far too often have simply told students, "This is right and that is wrong" without providing insight into the fact that in language rightness and wrongness are relative and are determined by historical accident and by social pressures of the time.

Today's emphasis is shifting toward consideration of language as a social tool. That means, for instance, that students are helped to become aware of the large and constant impact of language on their lives, aware of the tie-ins between what happens to people and what happens to their language, and aware that linguistic differences are as natural, unavoidable, and even desirable as are differences in height, weight, sex, coloration, mental processes, interests, and beliefs. Here are examples of the thousands of possible ways to teach and learn about the human, social qualities of language:

Exemplify and discuss the "languages" of lower animals —birds, poultry, dogs, cats, porpoises, etc. Compare with the essential qualities of human language.

Imagine that inhabitants of another world, with a variety of communication unlike any here, arrive on Earth. How might we and they communicate?

In a unit on dialects, especially those of people with non-Anglo-Saxon heritage, combine study of dialectal differences with a review of the cultural contributions of the national and ethnic groups represented by the dialects; e.g., blacks and Spanish-speaking people have contributed greatly to the development of America.

In the study of lexicography, humanize with a little biographical investigation of great lexicographers like Johnson and Webster, not omitting some of the anecdotes about their eccentricities.

Emphasize that the prime function of language is to communicate and thus to link one person with others. Only hermits exist without talking with or writing to others.

The stories behind many words reflect human beings and human considerations. Students may find unexpected humanness in *agony, ambition, candidate, curfew, extravagant, inaugurate, milliner, recalcitrant, rival,* and many more, as well as in the scores of words based on people's names, like *dahlia, derrick, platonic, watt.*

In studying the history of the language, find out how English happened to borrow more than 90 percent of its vocabulary from other languages, including considerable numbers of words from French, Italian, Arabic, and other living languages. (Englishmen's physical, commercial, and cultural contacts with people from other countries were often responsible.) A brief look at examples of words that other languages are borrowing from us may also be of interest.

RELATING LANGUAGE STUDY
TO LITERATURE

In comparison with English classes of thirty or forty years ago, today's classes devote considerably more time to literature. Literary study, however, may be considerably enriched if as a regular part of it the class considers the language in which that literature is written.

Joseph E. Milosh, Jr., in his *Teaching the History of the English Language* (Champaign: National Council of Teachers of English, 1972, pp. 69 ff.) says that "there is much support for the theory that the study of language can improve the study of literature," although ways of integrating the two are as yet not "very fully or concretely developed." He points out that the history of English can offer help "on the simple level of understanding what a text literally says," since words may change in meanings over the centuries. He quotes from Janice Schukart, who uses snippets of recordings to show students what *Beowulf, Sir Gawain,* and *Hamlet* sounded like in their original pronunciations, and who looks with students at the "highly amusing" syntax of Mr. Collins in *Pride and Prejudice.* Milosh's book offers numerous other suggestions for correlating language study with that of literature and emphasizes "integration" of the two, not "mere juxtaposition." Here are some specific examples of how such integration may be aided:

Examine the use of dialects in writings like those of Mark Twain or Leo Rosten, observing the contribution that dialect makes to characterization and noting that the "good guys" are as likely as the "bad guys" to use nonstandard dialect.

A unit suggested by the Minnesota Project English Center concerns "the language of evocation," i.e., language that evokes an experience. Poetry, radio broadcasts, and other literary or quasi-literary materials written after President Kennedy's death are analyzed to see how they project emotions, and the class then moves on to less obviously emotional literary material for further analysis.

In the study of Shakespeare, some of his sentence patterns may be compared with those of today. For example, Shakespeare and his contemporaries made relatively infrequent use of the *do*-transformation in questions and negatives, tending to say "Whence came he?" and "He knows not" rather than "Where did he come from?" and "He does not know."

Brief attention may be paid to the gradual shortening of English sentences since the seventeenth century. For example, in Milton or the eighteenth-century Swift and Johnson, sentences of one hundred or even two hundred words or more are not uncommon, but in today's literature the average length is only about twenty words per sentence. What effects has this trend had on literature?

A comparison of the language of poetry and that of prose of a given era, e.g., the romantic age or our own century, may be interesting if not too long continued.

Milosh suggests comparing the language of Chaucer with that of a modern translation, "noting differences in word order and [word] endings, and going on to discuss the different literary effects."

Bits from experimental modern writers—the more avant garde the better—may be read to note the kinds of things they do with the language. (e. e. cummings is a good though obvious starting point.)

RELATING LANGUAGE STUDY
TO COMPOSITION

George Orwell wrote, "The great enemy of language is insincerity." Language, he said, "becomes ugly and inaccurate because our thoughts are foolish, but the slovenliness of our [use of] language makes it easier for us to have foolish thoughts."

The best teachers of composition have always stressed sincerity, which requires honest use of the most precise language the speaker or writer has available. In other words, good speaking or writing is that which is not merely "correct" but also has something to say and says it clearly, honestly, and directly.

The study of semantics, then, has for composition an especially great value. It deals with words—their meanings and their nuances. It helps the student to distinguish between the meaty statement and the hollow phrase, between honesty and dishonesty; it encourages him to try to eliminate from his own expression emptiness, echoism, mere glibness.

Other parts of language study have their own contributions to make. Grammar reveals—brings to the level of consciousness —the array of sentence patterns and other grammatical resources available. Study of usage, when it does not degenerate into hauling up cannons to exterminate gnats, enables the student to avoid choices ("between you and I," "has went") that would alienate many readers. One value of lexicography is that it can lead to more intelligent use of the dictionary. The study of dialects may lead the writer to eschew on some occasions, and to use in conscious styling on others, expressions of limited geographical or social provenance. And knowledge of language history affords a special richness, an informed quality that can show up repeatedly in the choice of a word, the shape of a phrase, the linguistic sophistication of an utterance; it can provide depth to writing just as knowledge of general history can provide depth to an analysis of a current event.

Some of the writing done by students can be on linguistic topics, such as Jonathan Swift's plan for an English equivalent of the French academy, the stories behind selected words, an analysis of a dialect used in a short story, an analysis of the language used in a group of television commercials, poems about favorite (or hated) words. Elementary or junior high children may enjoy writing imaginative accounts of origins: How Language Started, The Man (or Woman) Who Made the First Noun, The First Written Story, etc.

Instead of making grammatical analyses of textbook sentences, students may compose sentences of their own as examples of certain patterns or may analyze and classify sentences of their own. Professor Don Wolfe has recommended the writing of many examples of each useful but relatively unfamiliar pattern in order to increase its use by students. Cadets at the Air Force Academy sometimes spend time in discussing a large number of variant ways to express the same idea.

To become better informed about matters of usage, able students may examine the eighteenth-century beginnings of prescriptivism and then observe the similarities and differences of treatment in usage glossaries in several current high school and college composition handbooks. For example, to what extent do the textbook authors agree among themselves about what is "right" and "wrong"? Similar comparisons may be made concerning selected items discussed in books on current usage.

Semantics exercises: a) Write a composition urging someone to purchase a particular make and model of automobile (or something else). Then rewrite, without changing any facts, but this time dissuading the buyer. b) Write several versions of an ad for a soft drink. One version should appeal especially to young children, another to teen-agers, another to parents, another to retired people, and so on.

Effective procedures for teaching the language do not really differ greatly from effective procedures for teaching anything else. As always, the teacher's personal qualities are important, particularly his or her enthusiasm, liking for young people, ability to think quickly and illustrate vividly, knowledge of varied teaching techniques, and knowledge of the subject.

It is in the last item, knowledge of the subject, that teachers of the language are likely to be most deficient. Until fairly recently, few colleges and universities required any courses at all in the English language. Yet federally sponsored research conducted in the late 1960s by ISCPET (Illinois Statewide Curriculum Study Center in the Preparation of Secondary School English Teachers, a study in which twenty Illinois colleges and universities collaborated) resulted in these recommendations for teacher qualifications in language:

Minimal	Good	Superior
An understanding of how language functions.	A detailed knowledge of how language functions, including knowledge of the principles of semantics.	
A reasonably detailed knowledge of one system of English grammar and a working familiarity with another system.	A detailed knowledge of at least two systems of English grammar.	
A knowledge of the present standards of educated usage; knowledge of the levels of usage and how those levels are determined.	A thorough knowledge of levels of usage; some knowledge of social and geographical dialects; a realization of the cultural implications of both usage and dialect.	Sufficient knowledge to illustrate richly and specifically the areas listed under "good."
	A knowledge of the history of the English language, with appropriate awareness of its phonological, morphological, semantic, and syntactic changes.	

Partly as a result of these and similar recommendations, many of the nation's colleges and universities now urge or require that future English teachers take a minimum of two courses in the language. For those teachers who lack such preparation, either two or more summer courses or the equivalent in independent study is strongly desirable if they are to teach the language knowledgeably and richly and with maximum benefit to their students.

3 The English Language

Jewell A. Friend

A BRIEF HISTORY

In an age that is concerned with Man's flight through space, one may readily wonder where his future will lead him. To lives aboard space vehicles? To friendships with residents of other planets? To implementation or facilitation of shuttle service between planets by means of lasar beams or conventional vehicles? To new concepts of time, human relationships, values? What will be the nature of life in the twenty-first century? Perhaps no single indicator will answer questions about life and values of the next century as the language. And the best way to understand how language reflects such phenomena is to look back in time at its cultural manifestations, to recognize the influences at work on language, to recognize factors that contribute to its growth or decay, to understand its dynamism and variety. This is probably the major reason for teaching the history of the language. Students are thus helped to perceive their language as a reflection of their past, their present, their future, their Selves.

Spoken by over 350 million people, English is the most widely used of the occidental languages. In addition to its use in the United States and Great Britain, it has become increasingly important as a second language in other geopolitical areas. For example, it has become the language of instruction in the Philippines (although Tagalog is the national language and Cebuan and Ilocano are spoken by the majority); it is the *lingua franca* of speakers of widely diverse languages, as in India; it is taught by approximately seventy thousand teachers of English in the secondary schools of Japan; it has been restored in the high school curriculum of the Dominican Republic; it has been increasingly the subject of study in African and Asian educational institutions as contrastive cultural analyses have become more and more important. Since a few decades ago the learning of English as a second language in many countries (including the Soviet Bloc) has been urged largely on the basis of the need to be able to read scholarly publications, literature, and technical materials that are not available in other languages. In other words, a significant factor in the popularity of the English language has been the industrial, scientific, and technological progress that we Americans have made. Indeed, we have good reason to take pride in the popularity of English.

A second factor that contributes to the growth and spread of a language is territorial expansion. If the size of the United States were to remain the same for the future, the English language would still probably expand because of the promising future of the Western civilization. Civilizations appear to be established and to thrive in temperate climates where soil fertility is relatively good. Opportunities for economic development (as in the U.S., Canada, Australia, and South Africa) and for sustaining high standards of living lead to language growth as, indeed, they did during the seventeenth and eighteenth centuries with British colonial expansion.

A third consideration in language popularity, in this case English, is its linguistic character. Among the assets of English are its lexical variety (sharing with other Teutonic languages such as German, Swedish, Danish, Norwegian, Dutch, and Flemish both structural similarities and vocabulary cognates, it nevertheless contains many borrowings from the Romance languages such as French, Spanish, Latin, Italian, Portuguese); its inflectional simplicity (only noun plurals and genitives, third person singular present indicative forms of verbs, comparative and superlative forms of adjectives, and pronominals are inflected after a history of reductions of inflections); its natural gender (living creatures are masculine or feminine, all else is neuter). Among the liabilities of our language are its idioms, its lack of correlation between spelling and pronunciation, its dialectal variety.

But, where did this wonderful Modern English language come from? A glance at the chart below shows that English belongs to the Germanic branch of the Indo-European language family. Other important branches are the Italic or Romance (Latin —spoken by Romans—and its descendants—French, Italian, Spanish, etc.); the Hellenic, or Greek; the Celtic; the Balto-Slavic (Lithuanian, Lettish, Russian, Polish, Iranian, Slovenian); and the Indo-Iranian (Sanskrit, Hindi, Persian). The hypothetical ancient language from which all these languages derived, Proto-Indo-European, was probably spoken in North Central Europe about 3500 B.C. The chart reveals that English is more closely related to Dutch and Frisian than to the other languages within the Germanic branch (German, Yiddish, etc.). Thus, English belongs to the western subbranch of the Germanic group. Because it derives from the lowlands of northwestern Europe rather than the hilly South German regions, it is called a Low rather than a High West Germanic language. The Angles and the Saxons came from these lowlands to England and brought with them the Germanic tongue from which Old English developed. Comparative and historical Indo-European linguists agree that lexical, grammatical, phonological, and orthographic similarities can only be attributable to a common ancestor. The kinship of English to many other languages becomes clear when we note similarities in common words like *one, two, three, four, mother, daughter, milk, water, eat, be, bread, sun, moon, home, father,* and *brother.*

English	German	Dutch	Greek	Latin	Sanskrit	Old Irish
father	vater	vader	patēr	pater	pitar	athir
brother	bruder	broeder	phrātēr	frater	bhrātar	brathair

I. THE INDO-EUROPEAN LANGUAGE FAMILY

Proto-Indo-European

Centum languages

Satem languages

Hellenic — Doric, Ionic Attic, Aeolic — Greek (Koine)

Italic — Oscan, Umbrian, Latin — Spanish, Portuguese, Romanian, French, Italian

Germanic:
- East — Burgundian, Gothic, Vandal
- North — West (Old Norse) — East — Danish, Swedish; Norwegian, Icelandic
- West — Anglo-Frisian — Old English (c. 450–1100), Middle English (c. 1100–1500), Modern English (c. 1500–); Frisian
- German — High — Modern Standard German, Yiddish; Low — Old Saxon — Modern Low German (Plattdeutsch); Old Low Franconian — Dutch, Flemish

Celtic — Gallic, Gaelic — Scottish Gaelic, Irish Gaelic, Manx Gaelic; Britannic — Cornish, Welsh, Breton, Pictish

*Hittite

Tocharian

Albanian, Armenian, Balto-Slavic:
- Baltic — Lettish, Lithuanian, Old Prussian
- Slavic — West — Polish, Czecho-Slovak; East — Russian; South — Bulgarian, Slovenian, Serbo-Croatian

Indo-Iranian:
- Iranic — Old Iranian — Persian
- Indic — Urdu, Hindi, Bengali, Romany; Sanskrit and Prakrit

*Hittite is regarded by some linguists as descended, together with Proto-Indo-European, from a still more ancient language called by scholars Proto Indo Hittite

Language Programs

The basic vocabulary of English derives from Germanic sources, but borrowings from other languages throughout the centuries are also evident. Many of our technical and scientific words result from our knowledge of Latin and Greek roots which we borrow as new lexical items become necessary for us. Similarly, many of our synonyms for basic words result from borrowings. For example, *get* is from Old English, but *obtain, secure, achieve* are not. *Earthly* is traceable to Old English sources; *mundane, terrestial,* and *global* are later borrowings.

Phonological correlations with other languages and with English at earlier periods are also revealing. For example, the nineteenth-century German philologists, Jacob Grimm and Karl Verner, noted sound shifts and correspondences between the Germanic languages and others. (Detailed explanations appear in chapter 2 of Albert C. Baugh's *A History of the English Language* [New York: Appleton-Century-Crofts, 1957].) A summary appears below.

Steps: 1. IE bh, dh, gh   > Gmc ƀ, đ, 3 > b, d, g
        2. IE p, t, k,   > Gmc f, p, x (>h initially)
        3. IE b, d, g   > Gmc p, t, k

Instances: IE bh (L f, Gr ph) / Gmc b

L frāter / brother	L fundus / bottom
L fiber / beaver	L fāgus / beech
L flāre / blow	Gr phōgein / bake

IE dh (L f, Gr th) / Gmc d

| L fi(n)gere / dough | Gr thē- / do |
| L foris / door | Gr thygatēr / daughter |

IE gh (L h, Gr ch) / Gmc g

L hortus / garden	Gr cholē / gall
L hostis / guest	L (pre)he(n)dere / get
L homo / gome	L hædus / goat

IE p / Gmc f

L pater / father	L per / for
L piscis / fish	L ped- / foot
L pellis / fell	L pecu / fee

IE t / Gmc p

L trēs	/ three	L tenuis	/ thin
L tōrrere	/ thirst	L tumēre	/ thumb
L tu	/ thou	L tonāre	/ thunder

IE k / Gmc h

L cornū	/ horn	L quod	/ what
L cord-	/ heart	L caput	/ head
L cent-	/ hund(red)	L canis	/ hound

IE b / Gmc p

Gr kannabis / ON hampr	L turba / thorp (-thorp)	

IE d / Gmc t

L duo	/ two	Gr drys	/ tree
L dentis	/ tooth	L decem	/ ten
L domāre	/ tame	L edere	/ eat

IE g / Gmc k

L genu	/ knee	Gr gynē	/queen, quean
L ager	/ acre	L grānum	/ corn
L (g)noscere	/ know, can	L genus	/ kin

Textual similarities are apparent in the following fourth-century Gothic, Old Norse, and later ninth-century Old English (West Saxon dialect) productions of the Lord's Prayer.

Gothic: Atta unsar þu in himinam, weihnai nano þein. Qimai þiudinassus þeins. Wairþai wilja þeins, swe in himina jah ana airþai. Hlaif unsarane þana sinteinan gif uns himma daga. Jah aflet uns þatei skulans sijaima, swaswe jah weis afletam þam skulam unsarain. Jah ni briggais uns in fraistubnjai, ak lausei uns af þamma ubilin.

Old Norse: faþer varr, sa þu ert i hifne, helgesk nafn þitt. Til kome þitt rike. Verþe þinn vile, sua a iorþ sem a hifne. Gef oss i dag vart dagligt brauþ. Ok fyrerlat oss ossar skulder, sua sem ver fyrerlatom ossom skuldo-nautom. Ok inn leiþ oss eige i freistne. Heldr frels þu oss af illo.

Old English: Fæder ūre þū þe eart on hoefonum, sī þīn nama gehālgod. Tō becume þīn rice. Geweorþe þīn willa on eorþan swā swā on hoefonum. Ūrne gedæghwāmlīcan hlāf syle ūs tō dæg. And forgyf ūs ūre gyltas, swā swā we forgyfþ ūrum gyltendum. And ne gelǣd þū ūs on costnunge, ac ālȳs ūs of yfele. Sōþlīce.

It is interesting to note that English in its origins was spoken by no more than a few thousand Angles and Saxons who invaded the territory now called England (land of the Angles). Like Latin and Modern German, Old English (OE) was highly inflected. An examination of the Old English passage above reveals that not only have spelling and pronunciation changed, but inflectional losses have occurred as well. Cognates for our words *father, our, thou, art, heaven, thine, name,* and *hallowed* are obvious. Words such as *will, earth, heaven, today, forgive, us, our, guilts, we, lead,* and *evil* are also apparent. Other words have either dropped out of the language or have changed in form or meaning. For example, the word *rice* derives from the same base as the German *Reich* and our English word *rich*. The Old English *hlaf* is our current *loaf* ("our daily loaf" in OE has become "our daily bread") having lost its *h* and having changed in spelling and meaning. Inflectional losses are clear and indeed contributed to the simplification of words such as *gedæghwāmlīcan* to *daily*. Because the Old English, as a synthetic language, signaled meanings by inflectional affixes and showed correspondences among words and grammatical modifications by this same linguistic device, word order was of considerably less importance than it is now. Our language, in brief, has become not only simplified but analytic or noninflected. We now signal meaning by rigid word order (compare *John hit Mary* with *Mary hit John*) and by function words (prepositions, articles, etc.). No longer do we signal nominative, genitive, dative, or accusative cases for every noun, pronoun, and adjective in our sentences. (In OE there was also a separate inflection for pronominals in instrumental case.) Furthermore, some alphabetic characters are no longer in use (þ, ð, æ). Nonetheless, there are enough similarities that we can see clearly that the language we use today rests on an Old English foundation.

A comparison of Old English and Modern English also helps to clarify some of the spelling inconsistencies that we often observe in our language. Some of the alphabetic characters that no longer appear in our writing system once served to signal distinctive pronunciations. For example, the "thorn" (þ) served to signal the "th-sound" as in the word *thigh* or *thing*; the "eth" (ð) signaled the voiced "th-sound" as in *this, that,* or *those*. The "asch" (æ) signaled the a vowel sound as in our modern *at, ash,* or *bat*. Other examples of vanishing sounds that remain in our orthography are *gnaw* (OE ḡnagen), *gnat* (OE gnæt), *knight* (OE cniht), and *climb* (OE climban). Between the fifteenth and the nineteenth centuries there also occurred a "Great Vowel Shift" which involved pronunciation changes in long vowels especially. Nevertheless, our spelling system, characteristically conservative, remained the same as it had become by the Middle English period. (It was during this period, 1100–1500, that the French scribes and French-trained scribes who occupied the British Isles made certain alterations in OE spelling.) Thus, the following modifications among others occurred:

OE	MnE
hūs	house
īs	ice
dōm	doom
stān	stone

Generally, our spelling system reflects the pronunciation of some five hundred years ago. But, a few examples of historical change may at least justify etymologically some apparent inconsistencies.

1. Expressions such as "six-foot long" and "two-mile wide" derive from logical earlier sources. OE speakers used "twa mila," *two of miles*, a genitive plural form. The *a* genitive plural affix became in time pronounced *uh* and was ultimately lost. The spelling changed to "mile" and the pronunciation became what it currently is. Thus, the word looks singular, but is historically plural.

2. Flat adverbs such as *hard* and *fast, soft* and *slow* are so-called because they lack the terminal *ly* that ordinarily signals adverbs. OE adverbs were formed from adjectives to which *e* or *-līc* (like) was appended. The *e* dropped away and the *-lic* was

thought normally to signal adverbials. Some adverbs resisted the pull of analogy and remained "flat."

3. The OE expression *Hit eom ic* (It am I) responded to the general growing emphasis on subject-verb-complement word order. Despite the fact that *Hit* is the complement and *ic* the subject, with the loss of the *h* in *Hit* that word was interpreted as the subject, and *is* was substituted for *am* (which evolved from OE eom) in the interests of subject-verb agreement. The final change replaced I (ic) with *me*, the objective form of the pronoun and the natural form to use postverbally. Thus, *It's me* evolved, and is acceptable generally.

4. The historical evidence of the acceptability of the double negative for intensification purposes appears in Chaucer's Prologue to the *Canterbury Tales:* "He nevere yet no vileynye ne sayde/ In al his lyf unto no maner wight." (He didn't never yet in his whole life say nothing nasty to no sort of person.) Because we no longer use multiple negatives for intensification, we also no longer accept these rhetorical forms as standard.

Some major influences on Old English were the Celtic settlement of the British Isles; the Roman occupations; the spread of indigenous populations into isolated dialectal communities; the Teutonic invasion; the advent of Christianity; the growth of and intermarriage of native and foreign groups; the Danish invasion and unification of Anglo-Saxon communities under Alfred the Great (ninth century), whose *Anglo-Saxon Chronicle* marked the beginnings of written English; and the Norman Conquest (1066) with the institution of French as the official language of the court and the retention of Old English as the vernacular. It should be noted that the French occupation after the Norman Conquest led to a rise of nationalism and a resistance among the British peoples to French or Latin as the lingua franca. By the end of the twelfth century, knowledge of English among the upper classes was common; knowledge of French, however, was uncommon among the lower classes. Interaction, however, necessitated bilinguality and the Anglo-Saxon language was inevitably influenced by Norman French.

SOURCES OF WORDS IN OLD-MIDDLE ENGLISH

Celtic (early origins, A.D. pre–449)
(place-names)
= *Kent, Devonshire, Cornwall,* Win*chester* (chester=Latin), Salis*bury, Exeter, Thames, Lichfield,* etc.

Latin (pre–43 B.C. invasion)
(common home terms)
= street, wine, kettle, disc, chalk, copper, bishop, kaiser, Saturday, etc.

(43 B.C.–A.D. 575)
(place–names, political terms)
= Win*chester,* Chester, port, etc.

(A.D. post-597)
(religious terms)
= abbot, abbess, alms, altar, angel, disciple, deacon, dean, litany, organ, etc.

Old Norse (Danish invasion of the eighth-ninth century A.D.)
= sky, skin, skill, scrape, scrub, bask, skirt, shirt, kid, get, give, gild, egg, they, their, them, Grimsby, Whitby, Derby, Rugby, -son, etc.

French (A.D. 1066-1204)
(words expressing class and dialect differences)
= valiant, labor, beef, city, gentle, baron, noble, dame, servant, minstrel, etc.

The Middle English (ME) period is arbitrarily set at A.D. 1100 to 1500 during which time England was generally a bilingual nation wherein French was the language of the court, English the language of the common people, and Latin confined to the church rituals and record. But the English nobility gradually lost its property (real and personal) and its close ties to the Continent and an international rivalry between England and France soon became keen enough to incite the Hundred Years War. Nobility had to declare allegiance to England or to France, for after the Norman Conquest many of them owned land in both countries. The English nobility confiscated the lands of the Norman nobles not in residence and France followed suit. A. C. Baugh observes that had the English retained territorial controls over estates in France,

French may well have become the permanent language of England. There developed, however, among both the common people and the nobility of England a strong antipathy against "foreigners" and a sense of nationalism. If French cultural ascendancy and the French language persisted in Europe, they most certainly did not in England. Indeed, by the fourteenth century, English was not only established as the official literary language (with publications by John Gower, William Langland, Geoffrey Chaucer, and John Wyclif [whose translation of the Bible brought English into the churches also]), it was the language of the courts. The 1362 Statute of Pleading provided that cases should be pleaded, shown, defended, answered, debated, and judged in the English tongue —although they may be recorded in Latin. English was even returned to the schoolrooms in 1349 and was in general educational use by 1385. Major linguistic changes during the ME period within the English language may be summarized as follows:

1. Inflectional endings for nouns had almost completely disappeared except for genitives and plural forms.

2. Except for very few archaic survivals, English adjectives had become uninflected by the fourteenth century.

3. Inflectional losses led to greater dependence upon word order, pronominal referents, and function words.

4. Pronominals became simplified through reduction of final syllables and inflectional loss for signaling case, number, and gender of referents.

5. Verbs underwent similar inflectional simplification or loss and weakening of final syllables. The former minority position of strong verbs (those resisting the pull of analogy and so of regularization) became more appreciable. Many former strong verbs in English disappeared and many formerly strong verbs became weak—that is, regularized in past tense and past participial forms.

6. Grammatical gender became simplified to a state of "natural" gender.

Despite the social and political hostility toward Frenchmen, things French, and the French language, the influence on English of the Norman occupation was substantial. To begin with, English had remained the language of the common people and because change occurs more readily in spoken forms of language, the political occupation paradoxically provided a catalyst for simplified forms of the English language. But many borrowings from French remained a part of the English lexicon.

Governmental and Administrative Terms: empire, administer, government, majesty, rebel, allegiance, traitor, treason, royal, reign, scepter, authority, prerogative, sovereign, tax, subsidy, revenue, record, court, council, statute, treaty, repeal, etc.

Ecclesiastical Terms: sermon, sacrament, orison, lesson, passion, communion, confession, religion, theology, chaplain, cloister, sanctuary, chapter, miter, etc.

Legal Terms: fine, forfeit, punishment, prison, gaol, pillory, defendant, judgment, doom, crime, guilt, indictment, convict, condemn, assail, banish, pardon, etc.

Military Terms: battle, combat, defense, ambush, strategem, enemy, peace, arms, retreat, soldier, guard, spy, lieutenant, captain, sergeant, banner, etc.

Social Terms: apparel, habit, gown, robe, garment, attire, cloak, lace, pleat, gusset, buckle, chemise, petticoat, embellish, adorn, satin, fur, sable, blue, brown, scarlet, saffron, brooch, turquoise, amethyst, topaz, garnet, ruby, emerald, dinner, supper, feast, mess, appetite, etc.

Art, Education, Medicine Terms: art, painting, sculpture, music, beauty, figure, image, ceiling, chamber, turret, porch, choir, cloister, poet, rime, rose, logic, geometry, clause, gender, physician, surgeon, apothecary, malady, plague, pestilence, distemper, pain, leper, paralytic, contagious, anatomy, stomach, pulse, medicine, ointment, balm, poison, niter, etc.

Sixteenth- and seventeenth-century England was characterized by a revival (after the Hundred Years War) of scholarly interest in humanism and in Latin and Greek, which interest called for new terms to express new concepts (meditate, emancipate, allegory, prosody, confidence, clemency, catastrophe). The new spirit of inquiry that resulted in exploration and the discovery of the New

World, religious reform, the Copernican theory, the development of the printing press, popular education, and industrialization brought about a recognition of the validity of the vernacular and an expansion of the English lexicon not only because of a need for new terms, but also because of inevitable contact with other cultures, subcultures and their languages. So great was the impact on the language that two schools of scholars argued about the acceptance into the language of "strange termes." One of the purists, Sir John Cheke, argued that "our own tung shold be written cleane and pure, unmixt and unmangled with borrowing of other tunges" and joined the hue and cry against the more liberal "inkhorners." Rhetorical passions became extravagant, but neither scholars nor legislators can adjudicate linguistic change. Paradoxically, we owe to this period of controversy a number of words that today seem indispensable: autograph, capsule, denunciation, halo, disrespect, disability, allusion, atmosphere, emanate, jurisprudence, conspicuous, insane, malignant, impersonal, external, hereditary, thermometer, tonic, acme, anonymous, criterion, ephemeral, idiosyncrasy, lexicon, conjecture.

In brief, the linguistic spirit of the age was one of expansiveness, rhetorical embellishments, national pride, literary prowess, standardization attempts, and relative liberality.

Among the major contributions of the sixteenth and seventeenth centuries to our Modern English tongue are the beginnings of recognition of the value of the vernacular, the growth in popular education (the result of the rise of a middle-class merchant class which was suddenly affluent and anxious to see their children educated and socially mobile), the standardization of the orthography (whereas formerly Norman and church scribes had established no standardized spelling conventions), and substantial phonological changes (the Great Vowel Shift evolves). Reasons for this latter phenomenon are uncertain. Some scholars attribute it externally to intrusions of foreign tongues with contrastive phonological systems; others attribute it internally to natural causes such as anticipation, metathesis, phonemic loss, etc. (See "Lexicography," Chap. 4.) Essentially it involved a weakening of unaccented vowels, inflectional losses with concomitant assimilation or dissimilation. Perhaps it may best be illustrated in the following model:

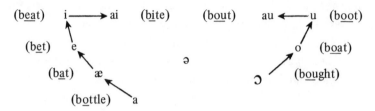

(b<u>ea</u>t)　i ——→ ai　(b<u>i</u>te)　　(b<u>ou</u>t)　au ←—— u　(b<u>oo</u>t)

(b<u>e</u>t)　e　　　　　　　　　　　　　　o　(b<u>oa</u>t)

(b<u>a</u>t)　æ　　　　　　ə　　　　　　　　(b<u>ou</u>ght)

(b<u>o</u>ttle)　a　　　　　　　　ɔ

The arrows indicate the general heightening of vowel sounds with fronting or backing. The vowel sounds (for those with relatively little familiarity) are indicated by the Modern English words in which they appear. The contrast between the Middle English (pre- or early-shifting period) and the Early Modern English (late sixteenth–eighteenth century) are presented in the following model:

Fourteenth Century	Seventeenth Century	Nineteenth Century
/fif/	/faiv/	/faiv- (five)
/medə/	/mid/	/mid/ (meed)
/kleinə/	/klen/	/klin/ (clean)
/namə/	/nem/	/neim/ (name)
/gɔtə/	/got/	/got/ (goat)

(An etymological dictionary will reveal in its phonological component many similar examples of pronunciation alterations for the period.)

Eighteenth-century attempts to refine and standardize the English language are discussed in some detail in the chapters on lexicography and grammar in this book. Obviously, standardization and codification of language are impossible by the very nature of a "living" language. If, however, one cannot fix a language, he can through publications and teaching standard forms retard linguistic change and infiltrations. But such a practice, as these early Modern English purists should have noted, leads to oversimplification of the rules of language and of the language itself, to

38　　　　　　　　　　　　　　　　Language Programs

pedantry, to affected gentility, and to linguistic elitism. Indeed, while Jonathan Swift would have welcomed the possibility of fixing the English language for all time (see Swift, *A Proposal for Correcting, Improving, and Ascertaining the English Tongue*, 1712), he saw it as an impossibility. Johnson, who "hoped in vain" for a purification of the English language, maintained that the establishment of an English academy to this end would be an infringement upon the principle of individual liberty. Any linguistic codification or change could only be affected by public consent, he insisted. We can see here the early seeds of our contemporary doctrine of educated usage as the desideratum. But to dismiss the plethora of grammars and treatises on usage by such eighteenth-century men of letters as William Loughton (*Practical Grammar of the English Tongue*), Joseph Priestley (*The Rudiments of English Grammar*), Bishop Robert Lowth (*Short Introduction to English Grammar*), Noah Webster (*A Grammatical Institute of the English Language*), Robert Baker (*Reflections on the English Language*), or George Campbell (*Philosophy of Rhetoric*) would be to misrepresent an age that worried about English forms and infiltrations. This was the period of development and expansion of the New World where American Indian terms, such as *skunk, terrapin, tomahawk, totem, wampum, wigwam, hickory, moccasin, moose*, were seeping into the English lexicon. This was a period of trade expansion and cultural diffuseness that brought into the English vocabulary such Mexican terms as *chili, chocolate*, and *tomato*; such South American terms as *buccaneer, jaguar, petunia, poncho, tapioca;* such Indian terms as *cashmere, china, chintz, mandarin, loot, jute, bungalow, calico, Brahman, cot, polo, punch, verandah;* such Australian terms as *kangaroo* and *boomerang*.

Nineteenth- and twentieth-century influences on our English language were wars (Napoleonic and Crimean, with France and Russia, respectively), expanding middle classes (with concomitant economic and cultural advantages), emancipation of slaves in the U.S. and the growth of black power (with inevitable and greater influences of blacks on standard English in this country—although the Afro-American's contribution to American English is historically demonstrable from the seventeenth century), the growth of science (with such neologisms as carbohydrates, enzymes, allergy, adenoids, hormones, stethoscope, electron, ionization, creosote, benzine, alkali, nitroglycerine, biochemical, radium, petrochemical, egocentric, psychoanalysis, inhibition, extrovert, inferiority complex, etc.), technological development (with such neologisms as carburetor, choke, clutch, gearshift, shock absorber, self-starter, steering wheel, bumper, hood, automatic transmission, convertible, station wagon, televison, ultrasonic, stereophonic, video, transformer, etc.), and wars (NATO, USAFI, bamboo curtain, flack, police state, iron curtain, cold war, jeep, foxhole, parachutist, paratrooper, crash-landing, blackout, task force, blitz, dive-bomb, air-raid shelter, etc.).

If a look at the history of our language tells us anything about English, it tells us that we can only speculate about its future in broad generalizations. We know how we came to speak as we do. We know what the influences have been and what they are likely to be on the changes that occur in a language generally. We know that, like morality, language resists legislation. We know that what we say and how we say it somehow reflect our heritage.

Exercises

A. Consider the following sentences in OE and MnE. What generalizations do you make about similarities and differences between the two forms of English?

> Stræt   wæs   brad   weg.
> The   street   was   Broadway.
> Mette he nænig guma þæt cuþe   West Seaxan sprecan.
> Met   he not any man that could West Saxon speak.
> Aeþelrud   is   min nama,   cwæþ   flotman.
> Athelrud   is   my   name,   said (quoth) the seaman (float-man).

B. Following are a few examples of English as it was during various early periods. How can we, using these excerpts from extant manuscripts, trace elements of change that have led to Modern English as we use it?

> ca. 1200: Nu, broþerr Wallterr, broþerr min . . . broþerr min i
> Cristenndom . . .
> Now brother Walter brother mine brother mine in
> Christendom . . .
> broþerr min i Godess hus . . . acc all þurrh Christess
> hellpe . . .
> brother mine in God's house . . . and all through Christ's
> helpe. (Dedication to Ormulum, London, 1200).
> ca. 1545: If any man woulde blame me, eyther for takynge such a
> matter in hande, or else for writing it in the Englyshe
> tongue, this answere I may make hym. . . . He that wyll
> wryte well in any tongue, muste folowe thys councel of

Aristotle, to speake as the common people do, to thinke as wise men do. (Roger Ascham, *Toxophilus*, 1545).

ca. 1550: On y dai Jesus comming from y hous, sat by y see sijd, and much compaini was gayerd togiyer, in so much y he went into a boot and set him down yeer. and al y hool compani stood on y bank. And he spaak unto yem much in biwordes and said. On a tijm y souer went forth to soow, and while he was in soowing summ fel by y wais sijd, and y birds cam and devoured it. and somn fel in stooni places wheer it had not much earth. (Cheke's, Gospel according to St. Matthew, 1550).

ca. 1618: He made a speach of more than halfe an howre, wherin he cleered himself of having any intelligence with Fraunce . . . more then to save his life and hide himself from the Kinges indignation: then that he never had any yll intent towards his Majestie. (Chamberlain's letter to Carleton, London, 1618).

C. What are some of the major influences on change in language? On pronunciation? On words' becoming archaic? On neologisms? On acronyms? On foreign words' infiltrating into the English language? On simplification of syntax? On inflectional loss?

D. Why is the selection of a "lingua franca" in new developing nations (such as those in Africa today) important? Note that the official language (lingua franca) is not necessarily the language spoken by most of the people. What are the social and political implications of such a situation?

E. There are many words that we could use in English that are not a part of our lexicon. For example, what do we call the inside of the arm where we get blood samples taken from—the part opposite the elbow? Invent an appropriate word. What do we call the clot of ketchup that forms to impede the flow from the bottle? Invent a word for it. When we refer to a group of people, including both men and women, we use the masculine pronoun to refer to a single member of that group. (Every *member* of the *committee* brought *his* own book.) (*Everyone* on the beach enjoyed *him*self.) (Any *teacher* or any *doctor* who does not protect *his* students or patients is negligent.) Invent a gender-neutral pronoun. Is there a nominative case for it, or only an objective case, or only a genitive, or one form to serve all cases? Why would the latter be preferable?

F. Have you noticed that the graphic forms of English-speaking writers other than Americans often differ from yours? Consider the number "seven" written 7 by some Europeans and Latin Americans. Why do you suppose this difference exists?

G. Check a good dictionary and determine where the following words in English come from: civil, citizen; organic, organization; store, storehouse; husband, hussy; humor, humid; master, maestro; fluorine, fluid, flour; marathon; khaki.

H. In some black dialects of American English, inflected forms are not in use. Indeed, sometimes (in very significant and meaningful ways) copulas (forms of the very BE) are omitted entirely.

My two brother(s) tell me yesterday you be coming.
John be working (meaning he is at work *now*). John working (meaning he is generally employed).

Indeed, George Wallace, former governor of Alabama, has been heard to say, "We not letting Washington tell us" (note omission of verb BE). The history of the English language reveals that it has consistently become more simplified (inflectional loss, omission of double negatives once used for emphasis, etc.). Do you think that black English is historically ahead of the standard English taught in schools today? Why? Why not?

I. What kinds of words might come into the English language as a result of War? Cultural exchange? Folk music? Chicano culture? Black culture? American Indian culture?

J. How many acronyms can you list in ten minutes? Why do we use acronyms? Do they make the language more or less "pure"? Is "linguistic purity" a myth? A desirable objective? Why? Why not?

K. Chart II traces the development of the graphic alphabet from ca. 2000 B.C. to the time of Christ. Remembering that the head of ox (a sacred animal to early Egyptians) was the first character in their ordered alphabet, what generalizations can you make from the objects that they used to represent in writing some of their basic ideas? Why do you suppose successive cultures modified earlier forms?

II. DEVELOPMENT OF THE ALPHABET

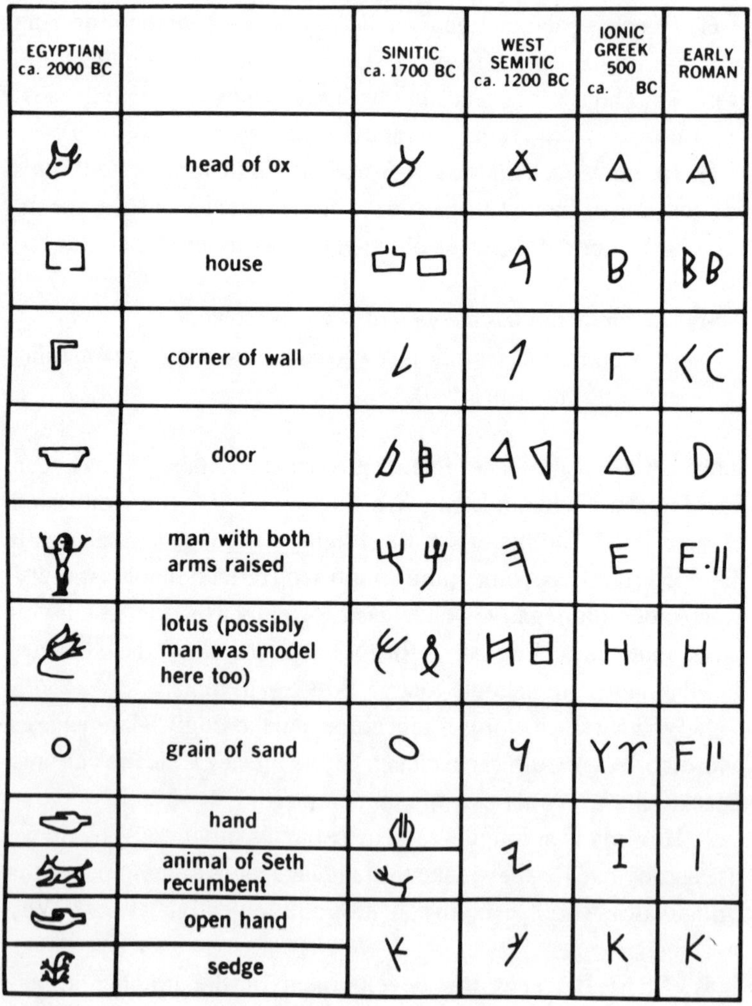
EGYPTIAN ca. 2000 BC
SINITIC ca. 1700 BC
WEST SEMITIC ca. 1200 BC
IONIC GREEK 500 ca. BC
EARLY ROMAN
head of ox
house
corner of wall
door
man with both arms raised
lotus (possibly man was model here too)
grain of sand
hand
animal of Seth recumbent
open hand
sedge

⬭	sandy tract, horizon (perhaps not origin of L)	?—o	レ⧸	∧	レL
〰〰〰	ripples (suggested also for N and even L)	⌃⌃⌃	˥	⋀	M
🐍	cobra	~⤻	˥	⋀	N ⋁
⬭🔸	ornament (often vertical) or weapon	=	IZ	I	Z
🐍	cobra				
👁	eye	⬭	○	O	O
⬭	mouth	8 ͽ	)	Γ	ΓԺ
⚒	animal's belly with teats and tail	—o	φ		Q
👤	head	⅌ ⑂	◁	Þ	R
➤	branch	ᘛ	⌄	⟨	⟩ ⟨
〰	sandy hills				
⊹ ⚲	unidentified cross or "ankh" the sandal strap	+ +	Τ ×	Τ	T

L. Consider the following summary of Rome's preoccupation with the Celts who once occupied what is now Ireland, Wales, Scotland, and England.

In 55 B.C. Caesar, in order to discourage Celtic aid to their Gallic kinsmen, invaded England and encountered spirited resistance. In 54 B.C. Caesar invaded southern England and established camps successfully, but he withdrew to Gaul when he failed in his attempt to exact tribute. In A.D. 43 the Emperor Caludius invaded and conquered southern and central England, a Roman conquest that lasted until A.D. 410. The Celts were driven north to the mountains of Scotland and Wales and west to the Isle of Man. During this four-hundred-year occupation, Romans provided baths, roads, heating apparatus, temples, theaters, irrigation systems, mosaics, pottery, dress, and ultimately Christianity. In A.D. 410, however, because of the expense of military occupation and because of barbarian invasions at home, the Romans withdrew.

In view of this historical summary, how can we explain the paucity of Celtic words in the English language today? What kinds of words would have infiltrated from the Latin tongue of the Romans? In what order—that is, domestic terms? military terms? names? religious terms? governmental and political terms? commercial terms?

 M. How might we explain the apparent failure of the italicized words in the poems quoted below to rhyme?

> Edmund Spenser (1552–99) "My Love Is Like to Ice"
> > My love is like to ice, and I to fire:
> > How comes it then that this her cold so *great*
> > Is not dissolved through my so hot desire,
> > But harder grows the more I her *entreat*?
> > Or how comes it that my exceeding *heat*
> > Is not allayed by her heart-frozen cold,
> > But that I burn much more in boiling *sweat*,
> > And feel my flames augmented manifold?

 N. The following excerpts from sixteenth- and seventeenth-century poetry contain words (italicized here) which once rhymed phonetically. Can you explain their failure to rhyme today?

> Robert Herrick (1591–1674) "Sweet Disorder"
> > A cuff neglectful, and *thereby*
> > Ribbands to flow *confusedly*. . . .
> > A careless shoestring in whose *tie*
> > I see a wild *civility*.

John Donne (1573–1631) "The Will"
>Then all your beauties will be no more *worth*.
>Than gold in mines, where none doth draw it *forth*;

Andrew Marvell (1621–78) "To His Coy Mistress"
>And yonder all before us *lie*
>Deserts of vast *eternity*.

John Milton (1608–74) "Lycidas"
>O fountain Arethuse, and thou honored *flood*.
>. . . that strain I heard was of a higher *mood*.

John Dryden (1631–1700) "A Song for St. Cecilia's Day"
>When to her organ vocal breath was *given*
>. . . mistaking Earth for *Heaven*.

Thomas Traherne (1637–74) "On Leaping over the Moon"
>O yonder is the *moon*
>Newly come after me to *town*.

O. Look in your town library and review its history. List any influences on the language of the people of your community that might be attributable to some historical event.

4 Lexicography

Jewell A. Friend

HISTORICAL BACKGROUNDS ON LEXICOGRAPHY: A BRIEF SUMMARY

Early dictionaries were designed to explain more difficult words in the language, not common parlance. This principle still abides in lexicography. For example, an entry that defines *ten* as two times five would be of little use. Similarly, a few people would be likely to seek out a definition of *kiss*, the entry for which might read, *to press with lips*. A brief look, however, at some of the earlier English dictionaries might place contemporary dictionaries and dictionary controversies in some perspective. In 1616, one of the earliest dictionaries of the English language was published. It was entitled *An English Expositour Teaching the Interpretation of the Hardest Words Used in Our Language, with Sundry Explications, Descriptions, and Discourses*. Its pretentiousness and prescriptiveness are obvious in the title alone. In 1668, John Bollokar edited the eighth edition of the dictionary which listed "most renowned persons; gods and goddesses; heroes of arts, science and faculties; terms from ancient history, poetry, philosophy and geography." The expansion of the dictionary makes obvious that its readership was limited to an intellectual and economic effete.

Seventeenth-century and eighteenth-century lexicographers saw a dictionary as an encyclopedic volume leaning toward Latinized jargons. They avoided plain English.

In 1617, Minsheu published *Ductor in Linguas* (Guide in the Tongues), an etymological dictionary with entries glossed in ten other languages. Ben Jonson called Minsheu a rogue because of his "research assistance and informants from Oxford and Cambridge" whom he supported financially. Minsheu was a devout philologist, however. Nonetheless, Jonson objected to Minsheu's speculations on etymologies many of which are now acknowledged in the *Oxford English Dictionary* (1921). For example, Minsheu speculated the word *dismal* derived from *dies mali* which translates *bad days* and the word *yeoman* derives from a contracted form of "young man."

In 1623, Cockeram issued his English dictionary, *Dictionarie or Interpreture of Hard English Words* proposing to "speed . . . attaining eloquent perfection of the English tongue." That lexicographers at the time saw themselves as arbiters rather than describers of conventional English seems clear. In 1678, Edward Phillips (John Milton's nephew) enlarged on the work of his predecessors with his *New World of Words or A General English Dictionary*.

Thomas Blount (of *Rehearsal* fame) published at this same time a glossary of neologisms and foreign expressions "now used in our refined tongue" chiefly intended "for more knowing women and less knowing men." Thus, Blount acknowledged (in addition to his chauvinism) foreign influences on and changes in the language. In the eighteenth century John Kersey reedited Phillips's dictionary several times and included many common terms such as *dog*, glossed "a well-known creature." The usefulness of such entries seems nil. In 1721, Nathaniel Bailey, who issued several editions of dictionaries, included an entry *dog*, glossed "a quadruped well known." His work became the standard edition until the publication of Jonson's dictionary. Bailey's 1730 edition omitted proper names and was the first dictionary in the modern sense of the term.

All lexicographers up to this time were characterized by pomposity, arrogance, speculation, lack of objectivity, and inconsistency in selectivity of items. With Samuel Johnson's compendium we have the first product of a literary man although he defines *patriotism* as "the last refuge of a scoundrel" and *pension* as "an allowance made to anyone without an equivalent; in England it is generally understood pay given to a state hireling for treason to his country." But Jonson's dictionary does cite various senses of words (134 for *take*); it exhibits a legislative attitude toward words, classifying some as "low, vile, barbarous, affected, of recent introduction," etc. For example, *budge, cooks, and swaps* were classified as low; *twittle twattle* was classified as vile; *wobble* was classified as barbarous; *chaperon* was classified as affected. Dialect words were included and treated sympathetically for the first time.

In 1844, members of the English Philological Society undertook the writing of the *Oxford English Dictionary (OED)*, completed and published in 1888 under the editorship of Sir James Murray.

The key to the authoritative position of dictionaries in America lies in our colonial history. The early history of our country, marked by separation from English speaking cultural groups, was characterized by certain insecurities regarding our folkways and our speech, our social graces and our lack of cultural prestige. Eloquence during the colonial period was closely tied to imitation of the way of life and language of the British gentleman. Indeed, Allan Walker Reed in his series on dictionaries in *Consumer Reports* (October 1963, pp. 488–92) points out that "We gradually sloughed off our colonialism . . . in manufacturing, in producing an American Literature, directing foreign affairs, but linguistic colonialism was the last to go. . . . The old habit of running to the dictionary remained, whereas an Englishman simply followed the usage of the people around him." The earliest American dictionary was published by Noah Webster in 1806. It was a small dictionary and was followed by an enlarged two-volume dictionary by the same author in 1828. His revision in 1839 sold very poorly, and in 1847 George and Charles Merriam, New England booksellers, bought the Webster manuscript. In 1893 Isaac Kauffman Funk, a journalist and publisher, issued *The Standard Dictionary of the English Language*, omitting detailed etymologies and emphasizing spelling, pronunciation, and meaning. All entries were alphabetically arranged. In 1893, Dr. William D. Whitney produced the *Century Dictionary*. This included a general literary vocabulary, technical, scientific, artistic, and professional terms. It also included pictures and encyclopedic information. In 1925, Sir William A. Craigie of the *OED* staff came to the University of Chicago to begin work on a historically based dictionary of American English. In 1944, this dictionary (in four volumes) appeared. In 1951, a revised dictionary of American English appeared in two volumes and was called *Dictionary of Americanisms* (automobile, christmas tree, congressional, bath tub, carpet sweeper, moron, sewing machine, typewriter, urinalysis were items included).

PRINCIPLES OF LEXICOGRAPHY

A. Not all dictionaries are the same or of equal value to all readers. When a lexicographer begins to compile data for a dictionary edition, he must make certain judgments about the size, the readership, the specific uses, and the priorities of his compendium. He must also determine stylistic criteria—the order of words, the order of preferred and nonpreferred spellings, alternate spellings, the order of definitions (generally in order of frequency of occurrence), phonological signals and diacritics which reveal standard or regional pronunciations, etc. Generally, however, reputable dictionaries consist of words, idiomatic phrases, combining forms, and affixes followed by information about their pronunciation, grammatical forms and functions, etymologies, meanings, syntactic peculiarities, variant spellings, conventional abbreviations, synonyms and antonyms, and illustrative quotations. An inspection of any good dictionary of English will make clear that in addition to the words which consist of one or more morphemes, it contains meaningful parts of words: suffixes like *-ness, -ly, -ism, -ize,-* and *-ment;* prefixes like *con-, de-, dis-, in-, mis-, pre-, per-, re-,* and *un-*; combining forms, chiefly Greek or Latin in origin, like *-gram-, -graph-, phon(o)-,* and *-tel(e)-.* It also contains conventionally called idiomatic phrases like *do in, make off, run down, black market, kick the bucket, pork barrel,* and so on. Little dictionaries, available in dime stores and drugstores, are not ordinarily very useful because they fail to provide, having sifted out for economy reasons, enough information on enough lexical items of significance to make them broadly useful.

B. Obviously, younger and less-advanced students need simpler dictionaries than older and more advanced students. Furthermore, every student should have easy access to a suitable dictionary at all times, in class or out. Ideally, every student should own a suitable dictionary, which means one of recent compilation and publication and reputable editorship, as well as one fitted to his own level of comprehension. Ideally, every class should have in it at least one suitable dictionary and preferably several of different editorships, so that information about words is always available during classroom work. And ideally, every school library should contain a number of good dictionaries of various levels of difficulty, both general dictionaries and specialized ones. Specifically, elementary school students should have a dictionary such as those issued by G. and C. Merriam Company or other companies under the Webster name and intended particularly for use by children of that level of maturity. There is also a good Thorndike-Barnhart elementary dictionary, somewhat differently organized. High school and college students need fuller wordbooks. The Merriam firm and the publishers of Thorndike-Barnhart dictionaries all offer acceptable books for use by secondary school students and the lower grades. More mature high school students and certainly college students should have nothing less than one of the five good "college edition" dictionaries currently available: In alphabetical order these are *The American College Dictionary, The American Heritage Dictionary, The Standard College Dictionary, Webster's New World Dictionary of the American Language,* and

Webster's Seventh New Collegiate Dictionary. The more recent edition and printing, the better the dictionary, for all of these books are constantly under editorial revision for the addition of new words and senses and for the elimination of errors.

C. No dictionaries of English contain anything like all the available information about the lexicon of modern English, let alone Middle or Old English. The largest of them contains about 145,000 entries—less than a third of the total vocabulary of modern English which has in excess of half a million items; no one really knows the exact size, for the good reason that new words are constantly coming into the language from many sources as new things, new processes, and new ideas come into existence. Hence, there is no dictionary that pretends to include all the words of the language. The largest and best dictionaries are the *Oxford English Dictionary*, generally known as the *OED*, and *The Merriam-Webster Third New International* generally known as *W-3*. For information about the basic word stock of the language, the *OED* is still our chief source. For information about relatively recent editions to the language, *W-3* is our best source. *W-3* is a one-volume work that can be bought for under fifty dollars; it should be in every high school library and certainly a number of copies should be in every college library. The *OED* is much more expensive but no college library should be without at least one copy of it, and the best high school library should have it. In addition to these books, there are the *Dictionary of Americanism* (*DA*) and the *Dictionary of American English* (*DAE*) to which the students should go for information about terms of specifically American origin or usage. They too should be in the library. And finally, there are the specialized dictionaries, such as Wentworth and Flexiner's *Dictionary of Slang*, Wright's *English Dialect Grammar*, and the many dictionaries of terms in anthropology, biography, chemistry, law, medicine, physics, psychology, psychiatry, and so forth. Some of these—certainly at least one good recent slang dictionary—should be available in high school libraries, and as many as possible should be in college libraries.

Lexicography

D. Students are more likely to use these dictionaries habitually and intelligently if they have learned how to use them in their classrooms, what to expect of them and what not to expect of them. It is advisable for teachers actually to read the introductory matter in these books so that they can explain to students how the material is organized, how to use and explain the apparatus so carefully devised by patient lexicographers to communicate their intentions. But, homework for teachers must precede dictionary homework for the students.

The printed dictionary exercises which are available from publishers at no cost and booklets dealing with standard dictionaries and their use provide helpful clues to dictionary work connected with reading, writing, and speaking done by students. But dictionary study must consist of more than exercises, useful as these are. The students should be expected to develop the habit of constantly looking in dictionaries for information about words. Whenever an unfamiliar word occurs in reading or listening, the students should look it up, learn what it means, and acquire other information about it.

These are familiar platitudes, nonetheless sound for their platitudinous familiarity. The best way to help the student to develop the dictionary habit is to arouse his curiosity and interest. Toward this end, the English teacher ought to have a sound grasp of the fundamentals of English linguistics; an understanding of the nature and history of the language, of how words and sentences are structured, of how standards of correctness are determined by actual usage, of the relation between nonstandard and standard usage and dialects, between formal and informal functional varieties. Without such knowledge the English teacher cannot do his job properly.

The linguistically informed teacher knows that a dictionary of English is not a sacred writ handed down on Mt. Sinai to Noah Webster or Sir James Murray or Phillip Gove. A dictionary of English is not an immutable digest of all English locution. Language changes constantly; Old English became Middle English, Middle English became Modern English, Modern English is not static. Yesterday's standard (correct) English may be today's non-standard or obsolete; today's nonstandard (incorrect) usage may be tomorrow's standard. Editors of contemporary dictionaries who know their business seek not to dictate but to record as accurately as they can the actual usage of the language, particularly among educated people in the conduct of their daily business. This means that the definitions, the pronunciations, and the grammatical labels recorded are those that conform to the facts at a particular time as determined by careful observation and documented by citations.

CONTROVERSY IN LEXICOGRAPHY

In 1961 the *Webster New International Dictionary* edited by Phillip Gove appeared on the scene. It had been preceded by an earlier edition (*W-2* in 1934) edited by William Neilsen, president of Smith College. Essentially, the *W-3* lists and accepts as "standard" words and expressions which *W-2* labeled "slang," "colloquial,' "erroneous," "incorrect," "illiterate." Gove has been accused of abdicating his responsibility as "custodian of the language." Unlike many earlier dictionary editors, Professor Gove sees himself not as a prescriber or arbiter of proper or conventional usage, but as a describer of the language as it is used by educated people. He acknowledges that language changes, that change is normal, that the spoken language is the primary language, that correctness rests on usage, and that all usage is relative. Dictionaries, he holds, are recording instruments, not prescriptive instruments. That he has not disregarded entirely those lexical items and expressions that have been in the language for a number of years seems apparent when we recognize that of over 600,000 items included in *W-3*, 350,000 consist of old entries from *W-2*, 100,000 are new entries and definitions, and 250,000 are quotations from contemporary sources. Gove has emphasized objective description, a recognition of regional phonology, a need for social and regional dialectal distinctions, and the relevance of quotations from contemporary persons in the public eye such as Jack Paar,

Art Linkletter, and Dwight D. Eisenhower. Obviously, none of these gentlemen, despite the prestige they enjoyed, is considered a scholar, literary or otherwise. Gove approved as acceptable English: *like* a cigarette should; to Mimi, *who* I love (noting that to many *whom* would sound like an affectation). Gove legitimized *finalized, anglicized, macadamized.* He listed terms as non-standard when *W-2* had characterized them as erroneous or humorous, e.g., *irregardless.* He deleted encyclopedic information. He was accused of tolerance of "crude neologisms" when he included such items as countdown, astronaut, sputnik, brainwash, megaton, occupational neurosis, blast off, sovietologist, megalopolis. Stylistically, Gove capitalized only God. Terms such as louisiana waterthrush, boston baked beans, new england clam chowder, philadelphia lawyer, new york city residence, edwardian work, he insisted on, in recognition of the growing tendencies of contemporary printing to lowercase nouns used in adjectival or adjunctive position. Stylistically, Gove used minimal punctuation and indeed no terminal punctuation. His definitions included as acceptable variants *each* usually singular—each of them is to pay his own fine/ *each* of them are to pay their own fines; different *than* or different *from*; *due to*—*due to* inclement weather.

Thus, *W-3* has become one of the most controversial dictionaries of all time. It has set a precedent for a descriptive approach to dictionary-making which has implications not only for the professional lexicographer, but for the English classroom teacher and for the students who use the dictionary.

Exercises

A. Using Donald W. Emery's *Variant Spellings in Modern American Dictionaries* (Champaign: National Council of Teachers of English, 1973), check spellings that are indicated as "preferred" in several dictionaries. If each student has his own, he will have to check the order of listings to determine if the preferred form precedes or follows the alternate. What does this tell us about the arbitrariness of spelling?

B. What are the running heads on the following pages:

p. 18   _____   _____
p. 109   _____   _____
p. 237   _____   _____

C. Checking the prefatory information, how many lexical entries appear in your dictionary? Does your dictionary contain proper names of persons or places? Does your dictionary contain foreign expressions that are used by educated speakers of English (*interim, sans pareil, persona non grata, iter ad astra, coup de grâce, coup d'état, caveat emptor, objet d'art*)? Does your dictionary contain slang terms (e.g., to *soak*— to overcharge, etc.? —See *socage* and try to determine the etymology of this slang term). Having done this exercise, speculate on the relative usefulness of the dictionary you own.

D. What is the date of publication of your dictionary? If language changes, how significant is this factor?

E. Check the etymologies of the following words and try to determine if there are any common features that might tell us something of their origin and development: *glisten, glow, glitter, gleam, glamour, gloss, glass*.

F. Linguists classify types of meaning-change as elevation (meaning becomes increasingly prestigeous), degradation (pejoration), generalization (meaning becomes more general), specialization (meaning becomes more specific and narrow). Words are also often classified as euphemisms (an expression regarded as less harsh), back formations (a word actually formed from, but looking as if it were the base of another word—*burgle* is a back formation of *burglar*), folk etymologies (a change that occurs in a word after prolonged usage and incorrect association with another more familiar form—*cold slaw* is a folk etymology of *cole slaw*), or neologisms (a new word or new sense of an established word or expression). Check the following words in your dictionary and classify them as one of the above eight categories: *curfew, dandelion, biped, calisthenics, goober, rodeo, undertaker, restroom, kodak, tycoon, uncouth, nice, cossack, kibitz, sauerkraut, villain, steward, marshal, alderman, hussy, terrific, bonfire, window, virtually, enthuse, nauseated-nausea-nauseous*.

G. Look up the terms *standard, nonstandard*, and *substandard* in several dictionaries. Do the definitions as they apply to English seem to agree? How do they compare with their definitions in *Webster's Third New International Dictionary*?

H. If one had to hyphenate the following words, where would he do so? Check your dictionary! *bedraggle, emphasis, multimillionaire, torrential, laboratory, prenatal*.

I. Which of the following words should be written as one word? hyphenated? written as two words? *doublepark, throwaway, sparkplug, goldrush, blackbird, scarecrow, seamark*.

J. Look up "Air Conditioners" in an edition of *Consumer Reports* and find the form and brief instructions provided for estimating the size of an air conditioner of a room. Require each student to select one of the eight sources of heat and join in a group to check that source in the classroom. (Some will check doorways, windows, overhead insulation, underfoot insulation, archways, legends on light fixtures or other electrical equipment, number of occupants, etc.) Using a dictionary and a tape measure or yard-stick, estimate the size of an air conditioner for your classroom. Students will learn to convert ohms, BTUs, joules, etc. They will have to use specific language to complete their task and the dictionary will be their major aid.

K. Underline the syllable in the following words that carries primary stress. *compromise, frequent* (two forms), *refuse* (two forms), *subject* (two forms), *accent, present* (two forms), *conflict* (two forms), *object* (two forms), *temperate, assist.* In the cases where two forms are indicated in the dictionary, what is the grammatical function of each? Why do we distinguish in pro-nunciation but not in spelling?

L. What is the plural of *mother-in-law? curriculum? stadium? index? bus? memorandum? formula? court-martial?* What is the singular of *data? criteria? cupola?* What is the past tense of *dive? leap? bid? cast? dream? sweep?* What is the infinitive form of *wrought?* What are the comparative forms of *dry? dreamy? good? gentle?*

M. How are the following words or expressions classified in terms of standard/nonstandard usage? *jimmy, galluses, fire sale, bully, cricket, lousy, joint, lid.*

N. What nouns and adjectives derive from *dinosaur*?

O. Many words in English are "borrowings" from other lan-guages. What are the sources for the following? *lariat, algebra, zenith, khaki, syrup, ukulele, guitar, guerilla, skunk, marimba, lorry, lieutenant, corral, kibitzes.*

P. The following words have interesting etymologies. Each student may take one or two and report orally his story of the origin of the word(s).

Humor	Enormous	Insect	Gossip
Dandelion	Husband	Woman	Names of Months
Weekdays	Naughty	Cliché	Unanimous
Partridge	Eccentric	Stupid	Music, Museum, Amuse
Starboard, Port	Heathen	Spendthrift	Supercilious

Colonel	Captain	Respire, Expire, Inspire	Proton, Atom, Electron
Don, Doff	Love (Tennis)		Carnival, Incarnation, Carnation

Sobriquet
Socage

Q. Why is *bombing* called *air support?* Check in your dictionary the word *support*. Are there parallels or inconsistencies in the use of *support* in the expressions *air support, financial support, moral support, political support, military support, legislative support?* If so, why shouldn't there be expressions such as *water support, land support,* etc.? Does the euphemism lie in the word *air* or in the word *support* in the expression *air support?*

R. Create a dictionary of euphemisms that might be helpful to a nonnative speaker of English. You may wish to categorize the entries in some way (morality, commerce, government, war, entertainment, etc.) Consider the following:

> It has a *mechanical defect*.
> Mr. Reilly *passed away*.
> Larry's father *succumbed*.
> That was a *costly error in judgment*.
> There was an incident of *social disease*.
> His wife was *expecting*.
> Were you *chubby* as a child?
> Real estate agents sell *homes* (not houses).
> They purchased a *homeowner's* policy.
> He became a *sanitation* employee, *chauffeuring* a department vehicle.
> We have provided *suggestion boxes* for *your convenience*.
> The child needs *remedial* help. He took *remedial* reading courses.
> The project, *negotiated by the government*, was *inoperative*.
> Is he *disadvantaged? Culturally deprived?*

He tried to justify his *fabrication,* but it was *counterproductive.*

The Watergate *incident* was the result of *inappropriate zeal.*

There was a felt need for *intelligence gathering.*

He indicated his *concern.*

Letter from the Ford Motor Company: "Continued driving with a failed bearing could result in disengagement of the axle and adversely affect vehicle control." (They recalled Torinos and Rancheros.)

Our troops in Vietnam made a *strategic withdrawal;* the enemy *advanced.*

The planes were *departing late* because of *a necessary change of equipment. Ground transportation* was available.

Remember that your glosses of the above euphemisms must be denotative, that is clearly defined in dictionary terms.

S. The "etymological fallacy" is an erroneous notion that the original meaning of a locution is somehow "better" than a later one. Words mean what they have come to mean, nothing else. They are quite arbitrary symbols which can take on various conventional meanings according to the uses to which they are put in a speech community. Hence, a word may in the course of time come to have a far different meaning from what it originally had. Check your dictionary for the following: *marshal, steward, buxom, pliant, lithe, hussy.*

T. The dictionary classifies words as *colloquial, obsolete, archaic, and dialectal.* Check the definitions of these terms. How does colloquial differ from nonstandard? Do colloquialisms have a place in informal writing? In informal speech? Do nonstandardisms have a place in informal writing? in informal speech?

U. Vocabulary growth in English depends substantially upon understanding the meaningful parts of words we encounter. Thus, *-soc-,* which occurs in *society, socage, social, asocial, associate, association, socialism, socialize,* etc., is a bound base—that is, one that doesn't occur alone—found in a number of frequently used words. The affixes *a-, ad-, -al, -ate, -ize, -tion,* and *-ism* are also common. Without using the dictionary at all, try inductively to determine what the base *soc* means in the constellation of words listed above. What might *vert* mean on the basis of judgment from *avert, advert, convert, divert, pervert, revert*; modified form—*vers* before *-ion* as in *aversion, conversion, diversion, perversion, reversion,* etc.?

V. Look up the words manageable, changeable, noticeable, and other words whose stems end with *ge* or *ce*. What spelling generalizations can you make about adding *-able*?

W. Practice writing some descriptive sentences using more precise words than you ordinarily use in speech. Describe the movement of a rabbit: does he walk, run, trot, scamper, dawdle, stalk, prance, caper, go, or hop across a road? Which of these words is more abstract? more specific? Describe a leaf: is it jagged, pointed, dentate, serrated? Describe a person: does he snicker, chuckle, laugh, giggle, or chortle? Is she coy, bashful, shy, or timorous? (Check a dictionary of synonyms if necessary.)

X. Check your newspaper and magazines for syndicated snippets of lexical information and begin a class collection to which each class member may contribute. (Starter: what is the difference between pants, slacks, trousers, ducks, britches?)

Y. Using your dictionary as a source, write a definition (denotative) of *rights*. How would you define *rights* etymologically? connotatively? illustratively (provide an example or illustration)? negatively (how, for example, do *rights* differ from privileges and prerogatives)? Use these data to write an extended definition of the "rights of the accused" or the "right to privacy"—note that the first is guaranteed by law (a statutory right), the second may or may not (a human right) be guaranteed by law depending upon the approach you take to the subject (your right to the privacy of your room, etc. versus the right of your family to protection from invasion by credit investigators, etc.).

Z. Most reputable dictionaries contain idiomatic expressions. Check the following "two word verb" expressions and try to determine whether these idioms would be clear to a nonnative speaker or if there could be ambiguities that might ensue.

run across	take over	put off	look up
run down	take down	put in	look into
run up	take in	put by	look down on
run over	take up	put over	look over

talk over	ask in	speak up
talk into	ask of	trace down
talk down	ask around	take time
talk around	call up	call down

What are the different ways they may be used? When are they particles? When are they prepositions? (Note that when they are prepositions, they must be followed by a noun or noun substitute; when they are particles, they are ordinarily separable from the verb.) How does the dictionary account for this peculiarity in English?

A. As you know, words change in meaning as people's experiences and use of those words change. Some words become more generalized. For example, note the following:

Butcher	once meant	goat-slayer
Companion		sharer of bread
Lousy		lice-covered
Average		damage to ship or cargo
Scene		tent, stage, covered place
Scorn		dehorn
Zone		belt
Pen		feather
Tally		stick of wood

These words have obviously experienced generalization. Check your dictionary (unabridged etymological) to determine how this might have happened.

B. The following words have become more specialized in meaning. Check your dictionary to determine why this specialization has occurred.

Lexicography

Starve	once meant	to die of any cause
Meat		food
Liquor		liquid
Girl		young person of either sex
Corn		grain
Etching		something eaten
Garage		a place for storage
Planet		wanderer
Malaria		bad air

C. The following words have become more elevated in meaning. Check your dictionary to determine how this elevation might have occurred.

Knight	once meant	youth
Squire		shield bearer
Chivalry		horsemanship
Chamberlain		room attendant
Constable		stable attendant
Governor		pilot
Paradise		park
Marshall		stable boy
Angel		messenger
Cathedral		cathedra, chair
Boudoir		sulking room
Jewel		joke, trifle
Shrine		chest, box
Silly		happy, prosperous

D. The following words have become less prestigious, that is they have undergone what is etymologically termed degradation. Check your dictionary to discover what might have been the process.

Lewd	once meant	unlearned
Knave		boy

Pansy	once meant	(from *penser*) "to think"
Smirk		smile
Wench		child, boy, girl, young woman
Awful		awe-inspiring
Diaper		valuable ornamental cloth
Scar		fireplace
Uncouth		unknown, strange
Sinister		left-handed
Gossip		godparent
Conspire		breathe together

5 American English Usage

Donald Nemanich

PRINCIPLES OF USAGE

A. Many people use the word "grammar" where "usage" might be a more accurate term. Usage as an area of language study deals with questions of social correctness and contextual appropriateness. Language scholars tend to apply the term "grammar" primarily to the study of language structure—word-formation, word order, phrase and clause structure, transformational rules, etc.; and "usage" to issues of "correctness" and standard and nonstandard varieties of language. "Usage" is in many ways a social aspect of English rather than a linguistic subject; "correctness" and other questions of usage are not determined by something inherent in the language but rather by emotional responses people have to various usage items. When most people talk about "grammar," they are really concerned with what is more accurately referred to as "usage."

B. Textbook rules of usage are often inaccurate or out of date. Dorothy Parker once insisted that anyone who used "none of those are" could never be a writer. The traditional rule to which she was referring stated that "none" is singular and required a singular verb, "is" or "was." Anyone who looked at the work of the major writers of the last two hundred years, however, would find that most writers have broken the "singular-none rule." And many other rules around since the eighteenth century are regularly broken by the best writers—"who-whom," "shall-will," end preposition, split infinitive, etc. In some cases, the rules were generally followed at one time, but usage has changed so that the textbook rules are no longer reflective of actual usage; in other cases the rules never did represent the general usage of educated speakers and writers of English but rather were merely creations of prescriptive grammarians. The eighteenth-century grammarian Robert Lowth created many of the best-known grammar restrictions based only on his own linguistic preferences and prejudices. Lowth condemned many usages found in Shakespeare, Milton, and the King James Bible. Many of Lowth's rules lived on for two hundred years in English textbooks while regularly being broken by almost everyone.

C. There is no single "correct" variety of good English appropriate for all occasions. "Good English" is a lot like appropriate dress: the wedding gown, swimsuit, blue jeans, pajamas, policeman's uniform, nurse's uniform, business suit, and lounging robe are all appropriate in some situations but inappropriate in others. None is inherently "correct" or "incorrect," "good" or "bad," "right" or "wrong." Each is simply "correct" or "incorrect" for specific times and places. Just as most people use different clothing for different occasions, so do most people use different varieties of language for different occasions—at formal meetings, with small children, in stores, at parties, at games, with good friends, with spouses or lovers, with strangers, etc. No variety of language is "good" or "bad" except in its appropriateness to the situation, the speaker or writer, and the audience.

Martin Joos in *The Five Clocks* describes five varieties or types of language that are widely used: *intimate* with a spouse or lover, *casual* with friends, *consultative* with strangers, *formal* for communication with larger groups, and *frozen* in carefully written material. Frozen language is not "better" than the other varieties; it just belongs in different contexts. One of the great mistakes

English teachers have made is to teach a single variety of formal written English as if it were the only correct style or register of English appropriate for any situation, when we should have more honestly been teaching the richness, abundance, and diversity of English and the many styles available to the speaker and writer. The user of English who is competent in only formal written and spoken language is in many ways as handicapped linguistically as the uneducated speaker who can use only nonstandard dialects of English. And he is even more likely to be an object of ridicule.

D. "Good English hits the mark." George Philip Krapp made this statement in 1909, but it is still a useful notion about usage. Krapp's point was that good English is not a single style, but whatever variety is most appropriate. A young man going from college into the army may find that polysyllabic vocabulary and standard usage are not always the best English. Likewise, a young person from the inner city may find it essential to use at least two different varieties of language, a nonstandard variety in the home and community and a standard variety in school, business, or the professions. The right language in each case is that which makes those communicating together comfortable.

E. Many scholars and reference works in this century have described three levels of usage—formal, colloquial, and substandard or nonstandard. According to this view, formal English was the variety used in most writing and in more formal speaking situations, colloquial or popular was used in friendly letters or in speech with friends or family, and nonstandard was used by the uneducated. One unfortunate result of this three-tiered view of language is that many people regarded colloquial language as something hardly better than illiterate rather than as a variety quite proper for many language events.

Formal

Colloquial or Popular

Nonstandard

F. In addition to "levels of usage," there are also "functional varieties." In an article called "Cultural Levels and Functional Varieties of English," John Kenyon argued that not only are there formal, colloquial, and nonstandard levels of English, but within standard English are numerous styles. Instead of considering formal as superior to colloquial or any other register being better than another, he considers all the varieties of standard English as being on the same level: colloquial, formal, casual, political, educational, commercial, scientific, technical, written, spoken, literary.

G. People judge others by the way they talk and write. We get impressions from letters or telephone conversations before we ever meet certain people. And when we meet people, we form impressions based on the way they talk—pitch, intonation, volume, speed, nasality, smoothness, word choice, fluency, grammatical complexity, pronunciation, and numerous other features. Probably we are never fully aware of how much we judge others by their language or how much they judge us.

Consider the Southerner who says "the las' time (tahm) you (yuh) tol' me, I (ah) foun' the nes' by (bah) the window (winduh)." Some may conclude that the speaker is lazy because he drops consonants or simplifies certain diphthongs. In a similar manner, when many people hear someone say "Ain't nobody know nothin' 'bout nothin'," they will assume that the speaker is either stupid or immoral or incorrigible. Often such judgments are totally inaccurate, but they are not unusual. Of course, language might also be "bad" by being too careful, too formal, too "prissy" for the occasion. A drowning man who called "I am in need of assistance" would probably get a laugh rather than a lifeguard.

H. Although considerable variation in language is acceptable and even desirable in our society, some words, pronunciations, and grammatical forms are nonstandard and should be avoided. Some specific items which are not widely used in standard English include the following: ain't, this here, don't have no, them books, leave it go, help Mary and I, he don't, wait for Mary and I, have went, have saw, have did, have came, have ate, have drank, have rang, etc., he help, he give, he done, he ask, he go, he begun, he run, he seen, he brung, he bring, hadn't ought to, try *and* do it, etc. This is, of course, only a partial list. There are other items that are just as clearly nonstandard. Such items are capable of attracting attention to the speaker in unfavorable ways. Many people will respond negatively to a speaker who uses expressions like the ones listed above.

I. Some items condemned by certain teachers and textbooks are widely used in standard English and should not be arbitrarily labeled "incorrect" or nonstandard. Unlike the terms listed above which are clearly nonstandard, there are other expressions which have sometimes been condemned by teachers or textbooks, but are in general use and considered standard by recent publications. The following, once questionable, are now generally acceptable:

> split infinitive
> "like" as a conjunction
> "different than"
> "guess" (suppose)
> "*fix*" (mend)
> "earth moved"
> "I couldn't walk any *further*."
> "You *had to have* property (in order) *to vote* in the
>   eighteenth century."
> "I don't know if I can."
> "Why *can't* I?"
> "It's *me*."
> "*Who* did you see?"
> "*Due* to his imprisonment, he found it difficult to
>   find a job."

None of these usages justifies spending class time trying to "correct" since all of them are now generally in use by educated writers and speakers. There are more important things to spend class time on.

J. There are some items on which various experts on usage disagree. The student or teacher who refers to two dictionaries, composition handbooks, or usage references may come up with two completely different judgments. Consider "the data is often inaccurate." Many older references will find this combination of

Language Programs

"data" and singular verb illiterate; however, most recent reference works consider this combination acceptable. "You are older than *me*," "you have been *proven* wrong," "*can* I go with you," "it is *liable* to snow," and "she was *enthused* about the project" are all debatable usages, acceptable to many writers and teachers, still objectionable to some.

Even with spelling, not all dictionaries agree. *Disk jockey, orangutan,* and *enology* are preferred spellings in two leading desk dictionaries, alternate spellings in two others, and not given at all in a fifth desk dictionary. There are several hundred words on which dictionarires do not agree on possible or preferred spellings.

SUGGESTIONS FOR TEACHING USAGE

A. Extensive use of workbook exercises should be avoided. The monotony of workbook drill is at least partly a result of the artificial examples out of any real context or natural situation. If on occasion some students need practice on certain items, the students should be provided with exercises on those topics without having the whole class going through the entire workbook.

B. Avoid negative, restrictive usage instruction. Provide stimulating opportunities for natural expression. Usage can be taught positively, encouraging students to use language naturally and creatively, in a variety of writing and speaking situations. Students should be taught the possibilities and options open to them rather than the restrictions of the traditional textbook.

C. As a teacher and grader, remind your students that "good English" consists of more than mere correct usage. Good English is appropriate to the writer or speaker, to the audience, and to the subject. Good English is also honest, clear, and concise.

D. Provide students with knowledge of how English is used in their world. Eventually they are the ones who will decide what kind of language they will use; therefore, the best thing the English teacher can do is to teach them about the possibilities of standard English and provide them with many different situations in which to use language effectively.

E. Standard English should be used and encouraged in the class without ridiculing the language of home and family. Attempts to obliterate the speech patterns of the community may lead to serious problems for the child and possibly for the school. Nevertheless, the student ought to learn that his speech patterns are neither the only nor necessarily the most effective ones. Standard English is an important means of communication in the larger society, and the citizen who can use it as a tool of communication has obvious social and economic advantages.

F. Usage items to be taught at each grade level should be selected with care. It is probably more effective to work on a small number of items thoroughly each year rather than to do a long list superficially. Correct tense forms such as "I saw" rather than "I seen" and the avoidance of the double negative should probably be taught before such items as correct pronoun case after prepositions or avoidance of "this here." Specific suggestions for usages to be taught at different grade levels are given in Robert Pooley's *The Teaching of English Usage* (pp. 173–215).

G. Instruction in usage should be based on the needs of students rather than on what appears in a textbook or workbook. No textbook knows your students or your community and their language needs as well as you do. You are best able to decide which language activities will help students become more competent and confident in English usage.

CLASSROOM ACTIVITIES

A. In one recent language textbook, the authors quote six different handbooks and other references on their treatment of "unique." Three of the books insist that "unique" cannot be used with a qualifying adverb—"very unique" or "more unique"—since the word "unique" means "one of a kind." The other three reference books are more liberal in their interpretations of "unique," suggesting that it means "rare" or "unusual," and thus can be modified by an adverb like "very" or "more." A useful activity in the classroom would be to consider such contradictions in authoritative reference works. It is beneficial for students to learn that in language usage, experts frequently disagree as to "proper" English.

B. In the Woody Allen film *Bananas*, there is a very funny scene with Howard Cosell doing a report on a political revolution in a Latin American country just as if he were reporting a sporting event. The humor of the scene is in hearing one variety of language where another is expected. An older example was Eddie Haskell on "Leave It to Beaver." With adults Eddie's language was always too formal. Discuss other places in films and on television where inappropriate language brings laughter.

C. John Wayne, Johnny Carson, Walter Cronkite, Barbara Walters, and Gerald Ford all use different varieties of language, each "correct" and appropriate for its user. Consider several well-known individuals such as those mentioned above. How do they differ in language use from one another? What are some of the characteristics of the language of each?

D. What are some vocabulary, pronunciation, and grammatical forms which annoy people? Students might find it useful to survey adults about those language characteristics which annoy or offend people. There are some items such as double negatives, "ain't," or wrong verb forms such as "I seen him when he done it" which are clearly nonstandard and generally avoided by educated speakers of English.

E. After a discussion of language usage, students may want to develop their own list of vocabulary, pronunciation, and grammatical items to be avoided in writing or in more formal speech stiuations.

F. What are some differences between spoken and written language? Consider, for example, sentence length, vocabulary, subordination, necessity for precision, punctuation versus intonation, etc.

G. Consider sex differences in language. What kinds of words and expressions are more typical of men than women? What kinds of vocabulary and grammatical forms are more typical of women?

Is it true as some linguists suggest that women use more adjectives than men do, especially words like "precious," "cute," "lovely," "exquisite," and "darling"? Is it true that in mixed groups men talk more than women do?

H. Discuss age differences in language. What words, expressions, pronunciations, etc., do students' grandparents use that they don't? What pronunciations, words, or phrases do young people use that older people don't?

I. A useful classroom activity for exploring the subject of different registers appropriate for different situations is to consider a single individual in a variety of different situations. Imagine a lawyer in the following places, for example: with his wife, with his small children, with his law partner, in court, at lunch on a business deal, at a school board meeting, with a clerk in a store, on a plane, making a political speech, at a sporting event, or on the golf course. Identify some differences in language between several of these situations.

J. What qualities differentiate the voice of a preacher on the radio from that of a sportscaster?

K. It is a valuable experience to present several sentences to a class typifying different varieties of language usage. The class can discuss the differences, including speaker, situation, and audience. Some possible examples are the following:

"He done told me."
"When shall we three meet again/
In thunder, lightning, or in rain?"
"I gotta read a short story tonight."
"One should be very careful when one is driving a car."
"You wanna eat at my house tonight?"
"The girl whose sister I'm dating's roommate is really pretty."
"I hear you not."
"Richard loves power more than Pat."
"Be he alive or be he dead/
I'll grind his bones to make my bread."

L. An inductive approach to usage in the classroom would let students describe language differences in different social situations. For example, the teacher might say, "You have just arrived at a party where you don't know anyone but the hostess. She introduces you to two people and leaves you to get to know them." The class could then be divided into groups of three to imitate this situation. It could be varied by having some groups be all teenagers while other groups have older people, people from foreign countries, famous entertainers, athletes, clergymen, politicians, businessmen, etc.

M. An English teacher might give each student in a class a different audience to speak or write to. One student could be given a bankers' convention, another the basketball team after a one-point loss, a third the mayor or alderman, etc.

N. To demonstrate language variation, students could be assigned to write about the same topic for several different audiences. For example, a student could be assigned to write several different notes about an assignment: first, a memorandum written to himself to finish an assignment; second, a note to a friend in another town explaining why he cannot visit over the weekend; third, a note to his parents about not wanting to get involved in a family outing over the weekend because of the project; and finally, a note to the teacher explaining why his project will be turned in late.

O. Provide the class with a variety of additional role-playing situations. Students might be assigned a variety of different roles—salesman, waiter, teacher, cashier, barber, politician, etc. They could then discuss differences in language appropriate to different people and places.

P. One of the most useful usage activities with adolescent English students is to have students examine their own varieties of language. They will be able to provide numerous examples of language differences with peers, parents, brothers and sisters, dates, teachers, sales clerks, possible employers, etc.

Q. "You have just received your report card and your grades are disappointingly low. Explain the situation to one of the following: your parents, your best friend, your boyfriend or girlfriend, a favorite teacher, a college interviewer, a counselor, etc." This oral activity provides students with an opportunity to consider language differences with different audiences.

R. Give each student a name tag to wear. The roles can include truck driver, aspiring actress, an elderly Englishman, a seventeen-year-old black girl from Harlem, a rock star, a Puerto Rican street-gang leader, a police detective, a rich brat, etc. The classroom is a party. Each student must act his role. He should make small talk using appropriate language. After five or ten minutes the teacher should ask such questions as the following:

1. Did your characters speak differently than they would have with peers or relatives?
2. Who did a good job of adopting appropriate language and mannerisms for his character? Who didn't fit his character? Etc.

Such activities should help students see that good English is appropriate to speaker, audience, and situation.

S. Pairs of students could take the roles of customer and waiter or waitress in a variety of restaurants—a greasy spoon, a McDonald's, a pancake house, a steak house, and the fanciest French restaurant in a big city. In each case they should attempt language and mannerisms appropriate to the situation.

T. After reading a short story like Shirley Jackson's "The Lottery," students might be assigned to write two letters, one to a newspaper editor about the events of the story, and a second to a close friend. The letters will probably be somewhat different in tone, vocabulary, and level of usage.

U. Students might try to collect examples of language from different kinds of television shows: comedy, police, game, children's, news, documentaries, soap operas. How do they differ? Are they appropriate? For example, do characters on soap operas sound like real people or terrible actors reading terrible scripts?

76   Language Programs

V. Have students do their own usage survey for a single item. They might ask people and also check dictionaries, English text-books, and usage references. The following items might be a beginning list:

Do it like he tells you.
I am taller than him.
It is me.
Can I go with you?
The toys were laying on the table.
They wanted David and I to read.
Everybody knew their jobs.
It is different than I expected.
The president has finalized the bill.
I will go irregardless.
She was really enthused about the project.

W. It was suggested earlier that appropriate language is like appropriate dress. A gown or tuxedo is not better than blue jeans, merely appropriate in different situations. What language situations can be compared with the social aspects of clothing?

X. To stress the idea that different ways of saying the same thing may be equally correct, collect examples of alternate ways of expressing the same ideas such as these pairs:

John was upset by the decision.
The decision upset John.

That she left early annoyed me.
Her leaving early annoyed me.

We gave the money to John.
We gave John the money.

In a hurry, Fred ran to class.
Fred ran hurriedly to class.

A Brief List of Resources

HANDBOOKS OF USAGE

Bryant, Margaret M. *Current American Usage*. New York: Funk & Wagnalls, 1962.

Evans, Bergen, and Evans, Cordelia. *A Dictionary of Contemporary American Usage*. New York: Random House, 1957.

Fowler, Henry W. *A Dictionary of Modern English Usage*. Edited by Ernest Gowers. 2d ed. London: Oxford University Press, 1965.

Perrin, Porter, and Ebbitt, Wilma. *Writer's Guide and Index to English*. Chicago: Scott, Foresman, 1970.

SURVEYS OF USAGE

Crisp, Raymond D. "Changes in Attitudes toward English Usage." Ph.D. diss., University of Illinois, Urbana, 1971.

Fries, Charles C. *American English Grammar*. English Monograph, no. 10. New York: Appleton-Century-Crofts for NCTE, 1940.

Lamberts, J. J. *A Short Introduction to English Usage*. New York: McGraw-Hill Book Co., 1972.

Leonard, Sterling A. *Current English Usage*. English Monograph, no. 1. Chicago: NCTE, Inland Press for NCTE, 1932.

Marckwardt, Albert H., and Wolcott, Fred G. *Facts about Current English Usage*. English Monograph, no. 5. New York: Appleton-Century-Crofts for NCTE, 1938.

Hartung, Charles V. "Doctrines of English Usage." *English Journal*. 1956.

Joos, Martin. *The Five Clocks*. Bloomington, Ind.: Indiana University Research Center on Anthropology, Folklore, and Linguistics, 1962.

Kennedy, Arthur G., *English Usage*. New York: Appleton-Century-Crofts, 1942.

Kenyon, John, "Cultural Levels and Functional Varieties of English." *College English*. 1948.

Pooley, Robert. *The Teaching of English Usage*. 2d ed. Urbana, Ill.: NCTE, 1974.

CURRICULUM CHECKLIST

Does your curriculum contain an inquiring attitude toward language, rather than rigid pronouncements of right-wrong, good-bad, correct-incorrect?

Does your curriculum emphasize many different kinds of language situations—spoken-written, formal-informal, rather than a single formal written variety?

Does your curriculum provided students the opportunity to practice standard forms and help in elimination of nonstandard items?

Does your curriculum help students eliminate nonstandard forms while respecting their homes, family, community, and culture where such forms may be used?

Does your curriculum reflect up-to-date attitudes of usage rather than out-of-date positions?

6 Dialectology

By Jewell A. Friend

DIALECTS OF PRESENT-DAY
AMERICAN ENGLISH (PDAE)

Perhaps the most useful of English classroom experiences for combating ethnic, regional, social, and linguistic provinciality and prejudices is the study of American English dialects. In pre-television days students were rarely exposed on any regular basis to any social or regional speech peculiarities other than those of their family and small community. Today, despite the pre-dominance of the Northern Inland dialect on radio and television, students do hear other American dialects on a fairly regular basis (country music—South Midland; teleplays—black, Southern, New England, etc.). Often, however, the contexts in which these dialects are heard deliberately encourage linguistic narrowness, misinformation, prejudice, and blatant cruelty. As one of the last hostels of humanism, the English classroom should help students to understand American dialects as manifestations of the color and diversity of English.

PRINCIPLES OF DIALECTOLOGY

Everyone of us speaks a dialect that is a product of our birth, parentage, social and regional environment. Some of us are bi-dialectal and can switch on cue.

A dialect, by definition, is a variety of a language spoken by a given community, regional or ethnic or social. Dialects, despite differences in pronunciation, grammar, and vocabulary, are mutually intelligible to speakers of a language. For example, New Yorkers and St. Louisans may differ on the pronunciation of the word *greasy* or *teacher*, or on the syntax of *I wanted (for) him to play on the team*, or on the word that describes a paper container (sack–bag–tote); nevertheless, their language differences do not impede communication because those differences are nonsignificant in terms of mutual intelligibility. When the variant forms (phonological, syntactic, or lexical) become mutually unintelligible, they are no longer dialects of the same language.

Speakers of the same dialect have individual peculiarities of speech and the term to describe the individual's composite speech patterns is *idiolect*. Thus, a dialect may be thought of as being composed of a number of idiolects, much as a language is composed of a number of dialects. Two large geographic dialects of English are American English and British English, each of which is, in turn, composed of a number of regional and social varieties.

Historically, some dialects have become more prestigious than others because they have been the speech patterns of leaders of communities. For example, the colonists who established residence in New England emulated speech patterns of the social, cultural, and political leaders of England. (Interestingly enough, the upper-class speech of London and the upper-class dialect of Paris continue to be the prestige dialects of British and French speakers, respectively.) Obviously, our Virginian ancestors disputed the New Englanders' claims to linguistic "superiority," and they maintained speech patterns of their own. (The Southern culture, based largely on agrarian economy and dependent upon slave labor, was inevitably to have its speech patterns influenced earlier by the speech of slaves with Africanisms and Americanisms.) As cultural and commercial centers developed (New York and Philadelphia), dialects emerged that were different from those of either the Bostonian or the Charlestonian. Indeed, there has never been an undisputed national prestige dialect in the United States. What did occur, however, was the spread of large cities and cultural centers in which prestige dialects, both regional and social, are recognized. Thus, one who seeks economic or social mobility does well in this country to recognize the differences among the acceptable speech patterns of educated and cultivated people in the various regions. (The English or speech teacher, therefore, is well advised to help a child to use standard speech of educated, cultivated people of that dialectal area.)

It is important to recognize that dogmatic assertions about "bad" or "good" speech are detrimental to the student. Slovenly, nonstandard speech should be corrected because it is as great a handicap to the student in society as is uncleanliness. To suggest, however, explicitly or implicitly that his speech is valueless or inferior is to threaten the identity of a student; changes in speech patterns to eliminate nonstandard forms demand understanding and cooperation. Regional peculiarities must be respected. There is nothing superior about *bahth, ahsk, nyews, Tyuesday,* or *neyether*; similarly, there is nothing inferior about *all (oil), tin cints (ten cents),* or *bucket* in lieu of *pail* if the student lives in the South Midland or parts of the Southern area of the country.

A major source of dialectal information is the *Lingustic Atlas of the United States and Canada,* originally edited by Professor Hans Kurath and later by Professor Ravin I. McDavid, Jr. This work began in the 1930s and is still in progress. In general, it maps out major dialectal areas of the country on the basis of field surveys and classification of informants with regard to age, education, rural or urban dwelling, and speech peculiarities (phonological, lexical, syntactic). *Linguistic Atlas* data reveal three broad dialect areas distinguishable in the New England, Atlantic states, and adjoining areas which define regions of colonial settlements. These areas are called the North, the Midland, and the South. The Midland is further divided into the North and South Midland areas. Each of these four dialect areas is, in turn, subdivided on the basis of peculiarities of speech and usage as shown in the following maps.

Language Programs

III. DIALECT AREAS OF THE UNITED STATES

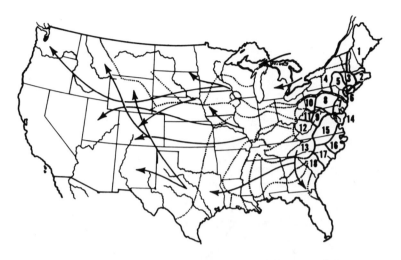

Atlantic Seaboard Areas (after Kurath). Tentative Dialect Boundaries. Arrows indicate direction at migrations.

THE NORTH	THE MIDLAND	THE SOUTH
1. Northeastern New England	*North Midland*	14. Delmarva (Eastern Shore)
2. Southeastern New England	7. Delaware Valley (Philadelphia)	15. The Virginia Piedmont
3. Southwestern New England	8. Susquehanna Valley	16. Northeastern North Carolina
4. Inland North (western Vermont,	10. Upper Ohio Valley (Pittsburgh)	(Albemarle Sound & Neuse
Upstate New York & derivatives)	11. Northern West Virginia	Valley)
5. The Hudson Valley	*South Midland*	17. Cape Fear & Peedee Valleys
6. Metropolitan New York	9. Upper Potomac & Shenandoah	18. The South Carolina Low County
	12. Southern West Virginia &	(Charleston)
	Eastern Kentucky	
	13. Western Carolina & Eastern	
	Tennessee	

The North comprises northeast New England, southeast New England, southwest New England, the Inland North (western Vermont, upstate New York), the Hudson Valley, and metropolitan New York. The North Midland comprises the Delaware Valley, the Susquehanna Valley, the upper Ohio Valley, northern West Virginia. The South Midland comprises the upper Potomac and Shenandoah, southern West Virginia, eastern Kentucky, western Carolina, eastern Tennessee. South comprises five dialectal subdivisions including Delmarva (a synthesis of Delaware, Maryland, and Virginia), the Virginia Piedmont, northeastern North Carolina, the Cape Fear and Peedee valleys, and the South Carolina low country (Charleston area). Historical explanations for dialectal differences involve influences of immigration, popu-

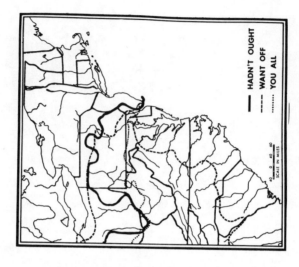

V. GRAMMATICAL ISOGLOSSES

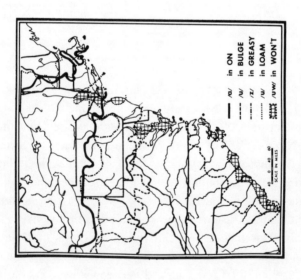

IV. PRONUNCIATION ISOGLOSSES

Language Programs

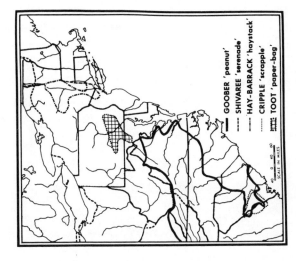

VII. LOAN-WORD ISOGLOSSES

GOOBER 'peanut'
SHIVAREE 'serenade'
HAY-BARRACK 'haystack'
CRIPPLE 'scrapple'
TOOT 'paper-bag'

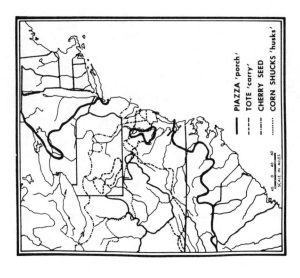

VI. VOCABULARY ISOGLOSSES

PIAZZA 'porch'
TOTE 'carry'
CHERRY SEED
CORN SHUCKS 'husks'

Dialectology

85

lation mobility, and relatively poor communication among various colonies. Generally, the westward expansion of these areas across the country (as populations moved) spread many of the patterns of speech in fairly symmetrical paths. As geographic mobility increased, however, Southern and Northern speech patterns influenced each other (particularly with the post–Civil War movement of blacks); and, the multiplicity of various Northern and Eastern coastal dialect speakers moving south and west resulted in what we sometimes call "General American." The following chart summarizes a few of the peculiarities of the various major dialectal regions.

AREA	PHONOLOGICAL	LEXICAL
North	with (voiced final consonant) *grease–greasy* (voiceless *s*) roots–roofs (/U/ as in *boots*)	*pail* (rather than *bucket*) *bag* (rather than *sack* or *tote*) *angleworm* (rather than *earthworm*) *frying pan* (rather than *skillet* or *spider*) *evestrough* (rather than *gutter* on roof) *dove* (rather than *dived*—past tense)
South	no /r/ before vowels in medial of terminal position (as in New York and Eastern New England speech) no intrusive /r/ (as in some eastern speech—*law*ʳ *and order*) vowel in *Mary, ferry* is /ay/ (unlike Northern Inland where vowel sounds *Mary, marry, merry* are homophonous) *Mrs.* becomes /mIz-*—rhyme with *whiz* *fountain* becomes *faountain* vowels in *your* and *poor* become *oh* initial vowel in *orange* rhymes with *paw* vowels in *house, out, bout* rhyme with *oat, boat* in Piedmont area of South	*bucket* (rather than *pail*) *tote* (rather than *bag* or *carry*) *carry* (sometimes used for *escort*) *you-all* (for second person plural) *goober* (rather than *peanut* in some areas)
Midland	*r* is pronounced after vowels (like Inland North) vowel in *wash, hog, fog* rhymes with *paw* final consonant in *with* is voiced *all, awl, oil* are homophonous in South Midland areas *can't* rhymes with *paint*	*bucket* (rather than *pail*, as in South) *blinds* (rather than *shades*) *skillet* (rather than *frypan* or *frying pan*) *wait on you* (rather than *wait for you*, in less-educated speech)

Language Programs

Social dialects in PDAE are generally more discernible in terms of pronunciation, inflectional and lexical and syntactic characteristics. Raven I. McDavid, Jr., summarized the significant features for discriminating social dialects as follows (in A. L. Davis, ed., *Culture, Class, and Language Variety* [Urbana, Ill.: NCTE, 1972]):

PRONUNCIATION

1. The distinction between /ø/ as in thin and /t/ in tin, /f/ in fin, /s/ in sin.

2. The similar distinction between /ə/ in them and /d/, /v/, /z/.

3. The distinction between the vowels of *bird* and *Boyd, curl* and *coil*.

4. The omission, in nonstandard speech, of a weak-stressed syllable preceding the primary stress, so that professor may become fessor, reporter may become porter, and insurance becomes su ns or so ns.

5. In nonstandard speech, a statistically disproportionate front-shifting of the primary stress, giving such forms as po-lice, in-surance, ee-ficiency, gui-tar, etc.

6. In nonstandard speech, heavy stress on what in standard English is a weak-stressed final syllable, giving acci*dent*, ele*ment*, presi*dent*, evi*dence*, etc.

INFLECTION

Noun

7. Lack of noun plural: Two boy came (come) to see me.

8. Lack of the noun genitive: This (is) Mr. Brown hat.

Pronoun

9. Analogizing of the /-n/ of mine to other absolute genitives, yielding ourn, yourn, hisn, hern, theirn.

10. Analogizing of the compound reflexives, yielding hisself, theirself, theirselves.

Dialectology   87

Demonstrative

11. Substitution of *them* for *those*, as them books.

12. Compound demonstratives: these here dogs, that (th)ere house, them (th)ere cats.

Adjectives

13. Analogizing of inflected comparisons: the wonderfullest time, a lovinger child.

14. Double comparisons: a more prettier dress, the most ugliest man.

Verb

15. Unorthodox person-number concord of the present of *to be*. This may be manifest in generalizing of *am* or *is* or *are*, or in the use of *be* with all persons, singular and plural.

16. Unorthodox person-number concord of the past of *be*: I were, he were; we was; they was.

17. Failure to maintain person-number concord of the present indicative of other verbs: I does, he do (perhaps the most widely recognized diagnostic feature).

18. Omission of the /-iŋ/ of the present participle: He was open a can of beer.

19. Omission of /-t, -d, -əd/ of the past tense: I burn a hole in my pants yesterday.

20. Omission of /-t, -d, -ɨd/ of the past participle.

21. Omission of the verb *to be* in a statement before a predicate nominative: He a good boy.

22. Omission of *to be* in statements before adjectives: They ready.

23. Omission of *to be* in statements before present participles: I going with you.

24. Omission of *to be* in statements before past participles: The window broke(n).

25. Omission of the /-s, -z, -əz/ reflex of has before been in statements: He been drinking.

26. Substitution of been, done, or done been for have, especially with a third singular subject: He done been finished. In other person-number situations done, at least, often occurs in standard oral English, as I done told you that three times.

The student who seeks social mobility can be led readily to an awareness of the speech characteristics that identify educated and cultivated people in this country.

One cultural dialect the study of which is essential to any language program is black English. Among the linguistic myths such study might dispell are 1) whites and blacks may be distinguished by a blindfolded listener; 2) linguistic differences are the result of underlying genetic racial characteristics; 3) any black who grows up in a predominately white community will still speak black English, even without exposure to other blacks; 4) all blacks speak a single form of black English which is inherently nonstandard because it derives from a kind of "broken English" developed by slaves; 5) black English is chaotic in form in that it has no formalized grammar; 6) black English is not a dialect of "American" English but is a separate language because it is unintelligible to speakers of standard English. Let's take each of these fallacies and briefly discuss them.

1. When Northern whites have been asked to identify black speakers on tapes, they have been unable to distinguish black speakers from Southern white speakers. They have also been unable to distinguish black and white speakers of standard Northern dialects.

2. The speech organs of blacks, whites, and all other races are the same. There is no genetic or biological factor that either enhances or inhibits speech ability or speech patterns in any normal human being.

3. Speech patterns are a product of childhood environment. A black child adopted into the home of white parents will speak the dialect (standard or nonstandard) of his white parents. Similarly, a white child who lives in a black community with black parents or guardians will speak the dialect of his community. It is experience, not race that dictates speech patterns.

4. Origins of black speech constitute one of the major sources of controversy among sociolinguists and dialectologists. A major theory, however, holds that slaves brought to the United States were linguistically diverse and thus developed a pidgin speech that approximated the English speech of their masters. Certain phonological, lexical, and syntactic characteristics of African languages survived to become a part of the pidgin English and the more

elaborated forms that developed within isolated or expanded communities. Thus, a full and flexible Creole that contrasts markedly today with the black English we hear is the Gullah dialect spoken in a small community on the South Carolina coast. What information we have about the pronunciation and syntax of early black speech in this country is unfortunately based on attempts of linguistically uninformed writers to represent the Negro dialect. It is important, however, to bear in mind the fact that some form of pidginized Afro-English had to be established in the west African ports where trade, especially slave trade, was prevalent for centuries. (A good source of information is the *Florida FL Reporter*, the spring 1967 edition of which deals solely with origins and nature of American Negro dialects.)

5. The linguistic phenomenon referred to as black English (which is really black nonstandard English, black standard being indistinguishable from white nonstandard English) has indeed a formal grammar. Among its consistent phonological characteristics (discernible also in much South Midland and Southern speech) are:

R-lessness— (also characteristic of Southern, New England, and New York speech) *bar, yard, marred*, for wherein the lengthened vowel substitutes for the /r/; *peer, speared, share, cared, moored, stored* wherein the center glide / ə / replaced the /r/.

Teacher: Compare *pores, paws, pause, pours*.

L-lessness— similar in nature to r-lessness, but loss occurs especially after back-rounded vowels although elsewhere also.

Teacher: Compare *pole, poll = poe; help = hep; too, tool = two; Paul = Paw* (try *Paul Powell/paw pow*); *fault = fought*.

Consonant cluster simplification—
especially in terminal position.

Teacher: Compare *passed, past = pass; rift = riff; meant = men; band, banned = ban; mold = mole*.

Compare /-s, -z, / ð, θ/, /-t, -d/ clusters in *asks, axe, six, boxes, parts, besides, that's mixes, facts, road, rowed, kept, pooled, boot, big, beat–bead, bee*. (Note that where consonant loss does not occur, weakening does—that is, voiced consonants often become voiceless.)

Vocalic identification—
/i/ and /e/ often become indistinguishable as may /uh/ and /oh/, /ay/ and /aw/—often monophthong-ized—/oy/ and /aw/.

Teacher: Compare *tin–ten, spend–spinned, since–cents, peel–pail–pill, poll–pall, oil–all–awl–old, time–Tom, think–thank.*

Obvious correlatives with phonological variables will be the genitive forms of nouns (wherein /s/ or /z/ may be deleted), future contracted forms (where *I'll* will become *I* with loss of /l/), and the use of *will* for emphatic forms only. Among its consistent morphological peculiarities are:

Inflectional loss—
genitive forms and third person, singular, present, indicative forms of verbs have no /s/ or /z/ which characteristic is explainable phonologically.

Copula deletion—
omission of copula signals a distinction between habitual and immediate present tense.

Teacher: Compare *He be sick* (note uninflected form); *He sick*; *He be working yesterday*; *He work yesterday.*

6. The tendency of black English to simplify by inflectional loss and terminal consonantal loss, by copula omission and omissions where only redundance is served (*my two brotherø*), etc., is consistent with historical trends. Some students of language speculate that these may be characteristic of standard American English one day. This is moot, however. Differences in phonology, morphology, and syntax are not so great at this time as to make black English unintelligible to all speakers of standard English.

Exercises

A. To illustrate idiolectal peculiarities in individual students, draw a clock on the board with the hands indicating 4:45. Explain that a hypothetical accident has occurred and they need to report it. The general time is P.M. Students must complete the sentence "The accident occurred at quarter (*of, till, to*) 5 in the (*afternoon, evening*)." Continue to move the hands after students respond until you have covered five o'clock in the afternoon or evening, etc. (5:15, 5:25, 5:35, 5:50, 5:55, 6:00). At some point the individual students will change from afternoon to evening in their idiolects. Consider what factors (and whether duration of daylight, mealtime, etc.) may influence. If the student will try this exercise again at home, he may well find that even members of his family differ in this linguistic way.

B. Ask students to indicate what they call a big meal in the middle part of the day (or late in the day) eaten at home (or in a restaurant or as a guest in someone else's home) on a weekday (or on Sunday or a holiday). Now try the same exercise with a small meal. Variations may involve the quality of the restaurant (a hash house versus a fine restaurant) or the time of year (e.g., winter, when it grows dark earlier). This exercise may illustrate family dialectal peculiarities.

C. For many things in daily life, people in different parts of the country use different words. Interview a few people from other areas to determine if what they call some of the following differs from what students in your dialectal region call them.

Is your town officer a . . . selectman, trustee, supervisor, reeve, councilman?

Is the room at the top of a house . . . a garret, sky parlor, an attic, a loft?

Is a porch with a roof a . . . gallery, piazza, porch, stoop, veranda, portico?

Is a wall made of rocks or stones a . . . stone wall, stone fence, rock wall, rock fence?

Is a heavy iron utensil for frying . . . a creeper, fryer, frypan, frying pan, skillet, spider?

When you do the housework, do you . . . clean up, do up, redd up, rid up, straighten up, tidy up?

Does the sun disappear at . . . sundown, sunset, dusk?

Does the sun appear at . . . sunrise, sunup, daybreak?

Do you call a very heavy rain of short duration a . . . goose-drownder, gully washer, trash-mover, toad-strangler, lightwood-knot-floater, squall, flaw, downpour, cloudburst, or something else?

Are window-coverings with rollers . . . blinds, curtains, roller shades, shades, window blinds, window shades, or something else?

Is a separate building for storing things a . . . shed, smokehouse, storeroom, toolhouse, toolshed, wood house, woodshed? If the building is attached to the main house, is it a . . . lean-to, shed, storeroom, or something else?

Is a road with a bituminous surface a . . . blacktop, oiled road, pavement, hard-surface road, surface-treated road, macadam road, tarvia, tarvy?

Is the center of a cherry (or a peach, apple, apricot, etc.) a . . . pit, seed, stone, kernel?

Are fried, round, flat cakes made with white flour . . . batter-cakes, flannel cakes, flapjacks, flitters, fritters, pancakes, griddle cakes, hot cakes, slapjacks, wheat cakes?

What is your family name for your father? mother? members of immediate family collectively?

What do you call a short quiz that has been unannounced? a long exam announced?

What do you call the student who always makes A's on tests? The brain? Something else?

D. Assign "tag questions" to the following cues. Be sure to add them as you would normally say them, not as you expect the teacher to have you say them in formal usage.

No one wants another hamburger (do they), (does he)?
Either Jack or Ben (is, are) going, _____?
He has several pennies, _____?
The Queen Mary was a fine ship, _____?
The Queen Mary had barnacles on _____, _____?
   (add pronouns)
You ought to try harder, _____?
Your cousin speaks four languages, _____?
My father's only child is brilliant, _____?
Brutus, my dog, is growing fast, _____?
I have plenty of time, _____?

E. Have students write a paragraph of their own using a list of words that vary dialectally in pronunciation (greasy, root, roof, out, house, car, park, oil, all, girl, bought, better, just, Chicago, bad, man, bottle, airport, marry, Mary, merry, law and order, garage, Tuesday's newspaper, etc.). Let them, using a tape recorder and cassette tape, go around and record various informants' reading of the paragraph to determine dialectal differences. Try to find people from other areas (who grew up in other areas) and people of several races, but be sure they are native speakers of English. (Students must be warned to avoid background noises on their tapes which interfere with audibility.)

F. Using tapes available through NCTE (1111 Kenyon Road, Urbana, Illinois) play the tapes and review the handouts which delineate dialectal peculiarities.

G. Set up a scene (in a post exchange on an army base, for example) where people from all over the country may meet for a card game or a meeting of some kind. Have the students write a short sketch in which names and language will reveal ethnic identity as well as educational level and socioeconomic status. (You might try having students write a heckling incident.)

H. Have students listen to TV and identify linguistic characteristics of the private eye, the hero cowboy, the western villain, the folk singer. Why are such characteristics used by the writers and actors?

I. Have students listen to TV and read accounts in the newspapers or magazines to do a short study or report to the class on folk speech, the speech of protest, the speech of diplomacy.

J. Nonstandard usage and dialectal differences have always been with us, prescriptive grammars notwithstanding. Check Wentworth and Flexnor's *Dictionary of American Slang*, David Maurer's *Dictionary of Underworld Jargon*, Captain Jack Gross's 1811 *Dictionary of the Vulgar Tongue: A Dictionary of Buckish Slang, University Wit, and Pickpocket Eloquence*. What kinds of generalizations can we make about slang as a part of dialect? What are the pejoratives that are characteristic of your dialectal area?

K. What are the characteristics of the lyrics of modern folk music? rock music?

L. A part of the dialect of the region is its onomastics (names of people and places). Check yearbooks for your school for sometime ago. Note first-name patterns. Where do they come from (biblical sources, prominent people in history, contemporary heroes, etc.)? Check to find out why Illinois is so called. Why is your town named as it is? Outlying towns?

M. Make some observations about women's language. There is more tentativeness expressed in women's speech (expressions such as *sort of, kind of, fairly*). There is more likelihood for a woman to use a tag question (*It's a lovely day, isn't it?*). There is greater specificity in color terms (not red, but *cerise* or *rose* or *magenta* or *coral* or *carmine* or *cardinal*, etc.) What other peculiarities do you notice? Why do you suppose these speech peculiarities exist? What about women's social position brought this about?

N. Undertake a safety campaign or a campaign to raise funds for some school use. Hold panels, buzz sessions, interviews; prepare poster appeals, radio-TV-film presentations, artwork, street interviews, etc. What is the nature of campaign language —persuasive aspects of our dialect. What kinds of slogans work in our area but would not be effective in another area, even one with the same problem?

7 Grammar

Jewell A. Friend

Until relatively recently, grammar was understood by many teachers as it was by laymen to be little more than a series of rules for the production of sentences that would be socially inoffensive. Indeed, expressions such as "his grammar is dreadful" signaled that there had been some infraction of a social amenity. The grammar was understood to be (as was the English exercise) a kind of linguistic book of etiquette. And in most cases the grammar that was taught was the traditional classroom sort, a kind of watered-down classical method of language analysis. Many educators held that drills and memorization of paradigms (conductive to "mental discipline") would produce eloquent written prose and articulate speech. The contemporary attack on English programs for the marginal literacy of high school and even some college graduates has driven home most forcefully the fallacy of the old premises and assumptions.

PRINCIPLES OF GRAMMAR

Let us consider a few basic principles before looking at the modern descriptive grammars and at some of the reasonable methods and goals in the English language program.

A. Grammar denotes the systematic use of language, not social amenities or verbal courtesies. The term alludes to the inventories of sounds, roots and affixes, word strings (phrases or clauses or sentences) that are logically ordered within a given natural language.

B. Grammar does not enact laws for the conduct of speech. George Kittredge and F. E. Farley pointed out as early as 1913 in their *Advanced English Grammar* (Boston: Ginn, p. xvi), "its business is to ascertain and set forth those customs of language which have the sanction of good usage. If good usage changes, the rules of grammar must change. If two forms or constructions are in good use, the grammar must admit them both." In brief, a standard form is arbitrary; indeed, many modern descriptive linguists concerned with all levels of usage and with dialectal peculiarities assume that standard forms are mythical.

C. The study of grammar will not produce effective writers or speakers. Walter S. Monroe in the revised edition of *Encyclopedia of Educational Research* (New York: Macmillan, 1950, p. 393) reports that research and informed sources deny that any "mental discipline" may be attributed to a knowledge of formal grammar. He further denies that there is any transfer or functional value of an interdisciplinary nature to the study of formal grammar, that is, neither reading nor writing nor speech in either the native or a foreign language is favorably altered by a study of grammar. Braddock, Lloyd-Jones, and Schoer report in their *Research in the Teaching of Composition* (Champaign: National Council of Teachers of English, 1963) that the study of grammar may indeed have adverse effects on writing skills. In brief, there is little reason to believe that concerted grammar instruction has any utilitarian value. If the study of grammar has any worth at all to the elementary or high school students, it must be intrinsic; it must be a key to the ways in which humans mold, shape, and alter language to their needs and values.

D. Grammars must distinguish between written and oral forms. The traditional grammarians concentrated on the written forms because written forms are more stable and thus more readily lent themselves to description. For example, words fall into oral disuse more quickly than they disappear from written use. When a word is no longer useful to a speech community because of its relevance to the function and values of that community, it may well still appear in the writing of that same community. Written records are often historical and less bound temporally with the immediate concerns of a cultural group. Then, too, speech is generally less formal than writing and formal language is by its nature conservative lexically and syntactically. Formal language resists neologisms and is deliberate in discarding terms that may have become orally archaic. Formal language generally precludes contractions, slang, nonspecificity, among other stylistic "liberalities" (J. Friend, *Traditional Grammar: A Short Summary*, rev. ed. [Carbondale and Edwardsville: Southern Illinois University Press, 1976]). Thus, contemporary descriptive grammars which emphasize the spoken forms of the language set for themselves a task that necessitates a synchronic pretension. In short, the structuralists and transformationalists must pretend their spoken language is not, in fact, changing at a given moment subject to their description.

E. Grammar, if it must be taught, is best scheduled for brief periods of instruction over the course of the students' total academic experience. Reinforcement of a grammatical principle then may occur as need arises in connection with other language study. (See chapters on "General Pedagogy" and "American English Usage.")

F. Grammars differ in terms of their purposes, objectives, methods, emphases. The following summary will serve to contrast some of the major distinctions among the three major approaches to grammatical analysis. Note that the numbered characteristics of each are parallel to that numbered characteristic of the other two so that comparisons or contrasts are clear.

TRADITIONAL GRAMMAR

1. The traditional grammarian saw himself as a prescriptivist, that is, he determined that his function was to adjudicate for

Language Programs

the lay public just how the language should be properly used.

2. He posited absolute forms of the language, forms that were correct or incorrect under any circumstances. He took upon himself to determine a hierarchy of effectiveness that would enable a literate public to use and to criticize written and spoken forms of the language.

3. Although he acknowledges the validity of other forms, the traditional grammarian concentrates on the more stable, written, formal language.

4. He recognizes that language is constantly in a state of flux but sees formal usage, wherein change is more deliberate, more enduring and thus more representative of proper forms.

5. As a grammarian, the traditionalist tries to find logical correlations between thought and language processes and patterns. (A sentence is a complete thought represented linguistically—that is, we think of "things" [subjects] and we make predications or statements about those things [predicates]. His approach is cognitive; he takes for granted a human linguistic intellect and is willing to speculate about it.)

6. Analysis begins with complete sentences and then involves subdividing successive units into two parts, binaries. (A sentence consists of a subject and predicate.)

7. The traditionalist uses the paradigmatic model. Following the Latinate formulae revered by eighteenth-century neoclassicists preoccupied with Roman and Greek culture and language, the traditionalist presents conjugations of verbs and declensions of nominals (nouns and pronouns).

8. The traditionalist classifies strings of words (phrases, clauses, sentences) and parts of speech not only in terms of their meaning but also in terms of their form. For example, *for harmony, to the other side, on a slope, by noon* are considered prepositional phrases because they begin with prepositions and are followed by a noun or noun phrase; they are all adverbial, however, because they signal purpose, direction, locus, and time, respectively. *When we arrived*, in the sentence, *When we arrived, the hostess greeted us with good news,* is an adverbial (dependent)

clause both because of its form—it contains a subject nominal and a predicate verb—but because it is introduced by a subordinating conjunction (when) which signals time. The sentence *Gounod composed "Faust"* is a sentence because it contains a subject nominal (Gounod) and a predicate verb (composed) and a nominal object (*Faust*). It is a simple sentence because it contains only an independent clause (that is, it can stand independently and be semantically acceptable). A compound sentence would contain two or more independent clauses (Gounod composed *Faust* and Joan Sutherland sang the female lead role). A complex sentence would contain one independent and at least one dependent clause (Gounod composed *Faust* in which Joan Sutherland performed). A compound complex sentence would contain two or more independent clauses and at least one dependent clause (Gounod composed *Faust* and Joan Sutherland sang the female lead role which was acclaimed a challenge to any soprano). Thus, the traditionalist defines and classifies parts of speech and strings of words both semantically (in terms of meaning signaled) and functionally (in terms of their syntactic and morphological form).

STRUCTURAL GRAMMAR

1. The structural grammarian sees himself as a descriptivist, that is, he determines that his function is to describe how the language is used by speech communities. He assumes no responsibility for making value judgments about the effectiveness of a language, but merely looks for patterns in a language.

2. He posits no absolute forms of language, forms that are correct or incorrect under any circumstances. He sees all language as relative to the needs of a speech community; indeed, his most reliable test is "the ear of the native speakers of a language." The language used by the uneducated is of as great interest to the structuralist as is the language of educated speakers. The formulae are the same; the subsystems (phonology, morphology, syntax) vary. There is, however, no hierarchy of effectiveness.

3. Although he acknowledges the written forms, his major

preoccupation in describing the systems (grammars) of languages is the oral or spoken forms.

4. Because most communication is oral and because all languages have oral (if not written) forms, the structuralist holds the predominant form of language to be speech which he considers "verbal behavior." His approach is, therefore, behavioral and he sets up formulae for "pattern practice and substitution drills." (See 7 below.)

5. The structural grammarian holds that to posit correlations between thought and language would be to make assumptions about thought and thought processes that are not demonstrable empirically. Only empirical evidence (sounds, morphemes, and syntactic strings) are admissible to the scientific analysis of language. Note that because he eschews meaning, the structuralist may undertake grammatical analysis of exotic and unknown languages which may remain unglossed.

6. Structural analysis begins with the smallest units of language, sounds (phones), and proceeds to larger units—combinations of sounds that produce meaningful segments —morphs, noun and verb phrases, clauses, sentences.

7. If language is learned behavior, basic structural patterns can facilitate the imitative process and simplify both the description and the acquisition of a target language. (This method was extremely useful during World War II when second language learning had to be achieved in short periods of time. It is equally significant now in intensive English programs and other "crash" programs in second language training.) Generally, a kind of frame-slot formula provides for vocabulary growth and pattern drills. Basic sentence patterns in English vary from linguist to linguist. Paul Roberts indicated four in his *Patterns of English* (New York: Harcourt, 1956); he indicated ten in *English Sentences*, (New York: Harcourt, 1962). Hook and Matthews indicate five in *Modern American Grammar and Usage* (New York: Ronald Press, 1956). Burt Liebert in *Linguistics and the New English Teacher* (New York: Macmillan, 1971), suggests seven as follows:

(Determiner) · Noun · Verb: Babies cry. The troops rallied.

(Det.) Noun · Verb · Adverb: The team plays well. John arrived early.

(Det.) Noun · Verb · Noun: I drink coffee. The boys played soccer.

(Det.) Noun · Verb · (Det.) Noun · (Det.) Noun: The usher handed me the ticket. They called him a taxi.

(Det.) Noun · Linking Verb · Adjective: We looked innocent. The collar feels wet. It appears dry. The students seemed interested.

(Det.) Noun · Linking Verb · (Det.) Noun: Jean became the chairperson. The concert was a success.

(Det.) Noun · Linking Verb · Adverb: The market was down. An officer was there.

8. Note that whereas the traditionalist defines and classifies parts of speech and strings of words both semantically (in terms of meaning signaled) and functionally (in terms of their syntactic and morphological form), the structuralist uses only formal criteria (a noun is a noun because it can follow a determiner, can immediately precede a verb, and may have a plural and genitive inflected form).

The __noun__ held a __noun__ in his __noun__ .

The child __verb__ a baton in his hand.

The __adjective__ child wore a __adjective__ suit.

He spoke very __adverb__ .

TRANSFORMATION GENERATIVE GRAMMAR

1. The transformationalist sees himself as a descriptivist, that is, like the structuralist, he determines that his function is to describe how the language is in fact used by speech communities. He assumes no responsibility for making value judgments about the effectiveness of a language, but merely looks at the alternate grammatical patterns in a language that express synonymous or ambiguous concepts.

2. He posits no absolute forms of language, forms that are

correct or incorrect under any circumstances but trusts the judgment of native speakers of the language. He sees all language as relative to the needs of a speech community but is primarily concerned with the oral and written forms of educated people. There are, however, in his system no hierarchy of effectiveness or value judgments.

3. Although he acknowledges the written and oral forms of language as worthy of analysis, the transformationalist is concerned with factors involved in choosing to express a single basic concept in one of a number of alternate patterns.

4. In opposing the structuralist view, which holds that scientific linguistic analysis must be formal, devoid of semantics, and based solely on phenomenal evidence, the transformationalist asserts that a linguistic description which ignores meaning, mind, and intuition is quite inadequate. A grammar must, by definition, involve semantic, syntactic, and phonological subsystems, for a language is a system that pairs meanings with phonic sequences.

5. Transformationalists view language as comprising a deep-structure (or conceptual) level, the nature of which is moot, a surface-structure level, and a phonological component. (There is general agreement about the last of these, but deep and surface structures are subjects of much controversy. One school holds that the movement from deep to surface structures can be effected entirely by transformations. Another school, the lexicalists, holds that transformations are necessary but that semantic features must be imposed on the items in the lexicon.)

6. Transformational analysis involves explanations of conjoining and embedding and of passivization, extraposition, aspect, tense, etc. This theory suggests a treatment of sentences with the same semantic content as variants of the same deep structure, produced by transformations such as relativization, reduction, deletion, and extraposition. It involves explaining processes, alternatives, and logical correlations between language and cognitive processes. Despite the insights into the relations between sets of sentences, and despite the pregnant notions of *competence* (basic linguistic knowledge—including intuition about grammaticality,

synonymy, and ambiguity) and *performance* (actual production of language, oral or written) discussed in *Language and Mind* (New York: Harcourt, 1968), Chomsky himself expresses skepticism about the application of this linguistic theory to language pedagogy: "I am frankly, rather skeptical about the significance, for the teaching of languages, of such insights and understanding as have been attained in linguistics and psychology. . . . It is difficult to believe that either linguistics or psychology has achieved a level of theoretical understanding that might enable it to support a 'technology' of language teaching" ("Linguistic Theory," *Readings in Applied Transformational Grammar*, Mark Lester, ed. [New York: Holt, Rinehart and Winston, 1970]. Obviously, flux, doubt, and uncertainty shroud the theory, and any teacher considering grammar text adoptions should do so gingerly.

7. If children produce novel utterances (as do adults in their speech) and if we all understand utterances we have never heard before and if we can agree on semantic ambiguities, synonymy, and grammaticality, then there must be a cognitive linguistic facility common to humans. Thus, language acquisition involves more than habit formation. To this end, the transformationalist takes semantically synonymous strings which are consistent with the Phrase Structure Rules of the structuralist and traces the linguistic choices (transformations) that produce these variant strings. For example, *Man build house* may produce the following variant strings when acted upon by one or more alternate transformations:

The man built the house.

The house was built by the man.

It was the house which the man built.

It was the man who built the house.

Was it the man that the house was built by?

Did the man build the house?

When (why, how, where) did the man build the house?

Combined with *House have cupola*, the above base component (Man build house) could additionally involve embedding transformations, conjoining transformations, etc.

The man built the house which has a cupola.

The house that has a cupola was built by the man.

It was the house with the cupola that the man built.

8. Parts of speech and variant structures are defined by the transformationalist in terms of both semantic (lexical) features and grammatical features. For example, the *data* would have the following features: +abstract, −human, −concrete, −animate, +nominal, +case, +number, +gender, etc. The first four "distinctive" features are lexical, the second four are grammatical.

Exercises

Probably the most effective way of teaching grammar involves an eclectic approach drawing on the major systems of language analysis—the traditional, structural, transformational generative. The system applied in a given instance will logically depend upon the linguistic premises, methodological procedures, and particular instructional objectives that are applicable and expedient. For example, to demonstrate particular bases for classifying words in a systematic way, a traditional approach may be useful; to point out the basic sentence types and patterns, the structural approach may be most useful; to illustrate alternatives in sentence varieties, the transformational approach (or some modification thereof) may be applicable. One pedagogic principle obtains: the student need not be a theoretical grammarian, nor should he be linguistically sophisticated; the teacher needs to be well informed in theoretical and applied grammars to teach English effectively.

A. Place the following nonsense words in some logical order and justify your arrangement:

> Quale detful onments vited argly.
> Velding achungs maparian the of clapt entism.

Which items look like nouns, verbs, adjectives, adverbs, articles, prepositions? Is each string a complete sentence? Why? Why not?

B. Using the strings of words above and assuming they constitute a sentence, write a phrase structure rule (formula) that would enable someone to produce a structurally similar sentence simply by substituting real words. For example:

    ag   snabs   refets   baned lainule nipers.
S—   Det + N   + N +   V-link + N   + N
    The Plains pioneers were mammoth hunters.

C. Combine the following simple sentences into one or more by conjoining (joining together) or embedding (placing one within another sentence) or appositioning (placing parts of sentences adjacent to others they most closely relate to—modify):

They were the first citizens of Illinois. They had entered a northwoods environment. There were forests. The forests were spruce and other hardy trees. Hunting was good, too. There were deer, elk, caribou, and giant beavers.

D. Make up a series of short sentences related in terms of subject. Then ask your classmate to combine them into longer sentences while you do the same. Compare your results. Is one more interesting than the other? Why? Why not?

E. Note that in the following sentences one sentence has been reduced to a single phrase or word. See if you can do the same thing with the sentences that follow:

Ex: Athena had gray eyes. She was the goddess of beauty and love.
    Gray-eyed Athena was the goddess of beauty and love.
1. Cattle gathered around rivers and salt beds to drink. Their feet beat the ground flat.
2. The plan had three parts. It was the one we preferred.
3. Illinois has many deeply buried paths of charcoal. They are the remains of ancient Paleo-Indian camps.
4. The Hopewell Indians lived in the Illinois-Kentucky Valley region from about 1000 B.C. to A.D. 500. They had a highly developed civilization. They were woodmen, hunters, farmers, and metal workers.

5. Lerone Bennett wrote a book which was called *Before the Mayflower*. It was a history of the Negro in America.

F. In 1968, the National Association of Afro-American Educators (Fact Sheet no. 3, August 1968, p. 2.) suggested the following definitions:

> A nigger—a person of color who has internalized a need to be disrespected by and to be subordinated to a person who happens to be white.
> A Negro—a nigger who desires to be like his white master without becoming too uppity.
> A black—a person of color who cleanses his soul of the need for masters—black or white—and who internalizes the needs to express himself in self-defined and humane ways by any means necessary —instinctively, planfully, and relevantly.
> Persons of color—niggers, Negroes, blacks, etc.

Using these definitions, what lexical and grammatical features could we give each of these terms to define and distinguish them? (±color? ±dignity? ±honor? ±self-respect? ±male? ±noun? ±animate? . . .)

G. Provide a word that fits the following descriptive features: −human, +noun, −abstract, +quadruped, +animate, −proper, +third person, −singular, +female =

H. Your community or one nearby has a local newsstand. Check it for magazines, look through a few on various subjects and for various readerships. What kind of differences do you see in the kinds of subjects? the kinds of words? the complexity of sentences? the numbers of pictures and their captions? Are captions in complete sentences?

I. Prepare a list of as many magazine titles as you can think of. Ask your parents and other members of your family to help you compile the list. Place the names of the magazines in categories that you set up by whatever criteria you think may be indicated by the titles of the magazines. In other words, what does the title of

the magazine suggest to you about the topic, appropriate readership, complexity of language, kinds of photography, etc. Your
categories may be activities (sports, gardening, hobbies, etc.) or
people (male, female, children, adults, teen-age, black, students,
teachers, bankers, farmers, etc.) or some other bases. After you
have done this, defend your report. What conclusions can you
draw about the language of magazines—verbal or pictorial?

J. Survey some aspect of community life and prepare a direc-
tory of consumer tips, a kind of comparative shopping report on
variations in price and product-value of items consumed by teen-
agers. Record shops, clothing stores, bookstores, entertainment
facilities, cosmetic counters, public facilities for seasonal activities (ski slopes or campsites, etc.) all provide valuable community
resources for exploration and well-designed reports. Notice that
your language will be relatively formal and perhaps even technical; it may involve jargon of trades and objectivity in language that is consistent with consumer reporting. (Class artists
may design a cover and thus explore the language of nonprint
media.)

K. A tag question is a short question that is tagged on to a
statement to turn that statement into a question. (It's cold out, *isn't
it*? She didn't go yesterday, *did she*? Your father drives a stake
truck, *doesn't he*?) Survey your friends and see which of the
following tags they would normally use? What does this tell you
about the practicality of strict rules of grammar?

No one wants another hamburger, _____ ? (do they?)
(does he?)

Either Jack or Ben is going, _____ ? (aren't they?)
(isn't he?)

He has several pennies, _____ ? (hasn't he?)
(doesn't he)

I've got plenty of time, _____ ? (don't I?)
(haven't I?)

You ought to try harder, _____ ? (oughtn't you?)
(shouldn't you?)

The *Queen Mary* sailed yesterday, _____ ?
The *Queen Mary* has barnacles, _____ ?
My cousin speaks three languages, _____ ?
My mother's only child is brilliant, _____ ?
He rarely takes this route, _____ ?
He often takes this route, _____ ?
He seldom takes this route, _____ ?
He frequently takes this route, _____ ?

Note that there may be responses you use normally in your language that do not appear in the parenthetical suggestions. Try to be as candid as you can in identifying your own ideolectal characteristics (your personal speech pattern preferences).

L. Listen to the lyrics of folk or rock music or country music. Why do you suppose they purposely use what many grammarians might call nonstandard grammatical forms of English? Provide examples and then try to put the lines in formal English. How would they sound? What is it about the "nonstandard" lyrics that makes them nonstandard?

M. Listen to a special program you enjoy on TV and make some notes about the language patterns of the actors. What kinds of special terms do they use that seem appropriate to the subject and the character they portray? Do heroic figures use nonstandard forms? How does their language help to convince you of their characterization?

N. Go to a restaurant or other public facility. What are some of the language cues (signs, greetings, speech of employees, etc.) that signal the kind of behavior (degrees of formality) they expect of customers or visitors or patrons? (Doctors' offices? Churches? Police Station?)

O. Make a note of theater marquees. What kinds of words are omitted from movie titles? What kinds of words are omitted from telegrams? What does this tell us about the kinds of words that carry the greater semantic (meaning) burden? What is the function of the other kinds of words? Is one group more important than the other? Why? Why not?

P. Write a story in a paragraph or two about a murder or a ghost. Tell your story in short sentences. Read it aloud to your class and note the tonal effect. Then, rewrite the story in long flowing sentences. Read it aloud to the class and note the tonal differences. (See example below.) What can we say about the usefulness of sentence variety to fiction writers? to advertisers? to essayists? to journalists?

> He clenched his fist. He pushed the door wide open. It banged against the wall. The doorknob splintered the plaster and chunks fell to the floor. He saw the light under the door at the end of the hall. He darted toward it. He threw his full weight against the door. It flew open. She was standing in the middle of the room. She lit a cigarette and blew out the light. She suddenly saw him. He aimed the gun at her. "This is it," he said. He heard the shot. She fell to the floor. It was quiet again as he left the room and walked down the dark corridor.

Notice that the last sentence is the longest one. Why is this appropriate? Do short sentences have a psychological effect on the reader? Can you describe the murder? Is the crime premeditated? Is it a crime of passion? How do you know? (How is grammar related to prose style?)

Q. How can you explain grammatically when you use *much* and when you use *many? ask* and *tell? some* and *any? this* and *that? these* and *those?*

R. Rewrite the following sentences to make them shorter and more concise. This is an exercise in what we might call "reduction."

> The trains were run by electricity.
> The planes had motors that were propelled by jet engines.
> He served spaghetti sauce that was saturated with garlic.
> It was considered a sin that was beyond forgiveness.
> The television program was for the service of the public.
> The general said that the troops were valuable but that they were expendable.
> It was land that had never been cultivated.

S. How can we explain in grammatical terms the way to use *remind, remember, recall, recollect*?

T. Grammars are not always grammars of language. Sometimes they are grammars (explanations of systems) of colors, music, totem poles. Get a picture of a spectrum and try to figure out what a grammar of color would look like? What would a grammar of music deal with? A grammar of totem poles? A grammar of some sport or dance?

U. Sometime in a hypothetical future dictionaries will be computerized so that we can punch plus or minus features on an index card and feed the information into a computer and retract the word we want—or even invent a new word. What kinds of features would be necessary to retract Homo sapiens (or femina sapiens)? *vacuum? gentility? poodles? hockey stick? light bulb? rattletrap? bee? isotherm?*

8 Semantics, Questions, and Language Exercises

Alan Lemke

Semantics enters language arts curricula in at least two ways—as a subject in its own right or as a set of principles supporting and influencing the teaching of language, literature, and composition. Junior-high and senior-high teachers show some interest in semantic studies, for they are familiar with the terms "connotative" and "denotative." *Concrete* and *abstract* terminologies receive attention and study; and often teachers' perceptions of the weaknesses of abstract language find their way into the advice given students whose compositions are vague, loosely organized, and trivial in thought. Less often, students are complimented for knowing the *powers* of abstract language. Some writing assignments lead students into the use of words closely associated with the five senses—sight, sound, smell, touch, and taste; these writing assignments often effectively reduce the number of clichés, high-level abstractions, and jargon so frequently found in students' "expressive" writing. As these examples suggest, teachers of English follow semantic principles implicitly in the teaching of composition, and teachers sometimes focus lessons on semantics itself. Semantics has not, however, received either widespread understanding or sufficient attention. This chapter offers ideas and classroom activities for those English teachers who wish to reinforce and move beyond the first levels of teaching semantics and composition in ways leading to student understanding of semantic principles.

Once known as the science of sanity, semantics purports to offer rational routes to solid reality, knowledge of reality, effective communication, and community sanity achieved through the use of concrete words are the components of an ideal universe in which discourse involves the effective use of semantic principles. Knowledgeable of the relationship between every word and its identifiable real-world referent, people could act sanely, humanely, and harmoniously. In the search for solid reality, for effective means of communication, for human sanity, and for harmony among all things, semantics often focuses upon the referents of words.

To most people, meaning is dependent almost entirely upon words having identifiable referents. Theoretically at least, a word without a referent is a word without meaning. Abstract words are most suspect; "education," "love," "trust," "sincerity," "justice," "equal opportunity," and "the American dream" are often thought worthless and meaningless because they are used loosely without reference to anything tangible, concrete, or stable. Liza Doolittle expressed for all of us the frustrations we have known when a lover, cruel Mother Nature, or an angry god breaks what we have taken to be the solidity of words and meaning. Liza's "Words words/words words words words words!/All I hear is words [*sic*]" (*My Fair Lady*) expresses the common belief that abstract words such as "love" are empty. Differences of opinion over the meaning of "poetry," "good poetry," "propaganda," "critical reading," "doublespeak," and "self-discipline" mark English teachers' distrust of words without referents. To have a meaning, a word needs a concrete referent, and words without referents have either no meaning or too many meanings. No wonder semantics is thought to be a science of sanity, for it ferrets out many words whose referents and meanings are vague or unknown. Like the semanticist, the teacher of writing abhors indiscriminate use of abstract words and advises the use of words whose referents are at least identifiable if not completely obvious. More than one student has seen "use concrete words" written at the bottom of a paper.

Unfortunately, advice that students use concrete words must be qualified and explained, for the referents of words are not always as identifiable as they seem to be upon first glance. The words "President Kennedy" apparently refer, or referred, to a man who held the highest federal office beginning in 1960. But what do the words "President Kennedy" refer to today? The word "pencil" seemingly refers quite clearly and simply to a pencil. Which pencil? Any pencil? The class of all pencils? To any member of the class of pencils? To what could "pencil" possibly refer in the question, "What is a pencil?" when asked by someone who does not know what a pencil is? Is the word "pencil" a concrete word in all cases? If there are uses of the word "pencil" when its referent is not known, can it be said that "pencil" has any meaning? And do intelligent and sane people use words whose referents are not identifiable? As these questions suggest, identifying the referents of words is not always easy. Some semanticists think it is impossible.

Some semanticists suspect that words refer to such mental events as ideas, images, and feelings—which are easier to talk about but no less difficult to find. Not only "President Kennedy" and "pencil" but also such words as "beauty," "run," "with," and "or" may very well have mental events as their referents. The referent for "beauty" lies in the mind of the beholder. The referent for action verbs lies not in an object but in the movement of an object or in a perceiver's conception of an object. Referents for prepositions and conjunctions are difficult to find either outside or inside the mind. Although it is difficult to find referents for all words, semantics offers reasons to believe that the meaning of a word is tied to the word's referential function.

As suggested above, even a brief consideration of very common and seemingly concrete words reveals a wide range of opinion about the referential function of words, about the wisdom of advising writers to use only concrete words, about semantics, and about clear thought and writing. The following exercises help students understand what it means to say "words refer to things."

1. Students can arrange randomly listed words into groups, depending upon the apparent presence or clarity of the referent for each word. The following groups suggest one way a student could handle the task:

Richard Nixon
Gerald Ford
John Gardner
Flip Wilson
Jane Fonda
(names of
living people)

Abraham Lincoln
Carl Sandburg
Martin Luther King
Sitting Bull
Janis Joplin
(names of non-
living people)

Maria
Lady Macbeth
Othello
Nokomis
Holden Caulfield
(names of
fictional people)

pencil
person
tree
atom
god
(class names of
objects)

density
force
color
mass
length
(class names of
physical qualities)

admiration
skepticism
objectivity
sympathy
indifference
(class names of
of attitudes)

conjunction
coordination
implication
negation

and   with
or   of
for   from
not   to
(others)

2. Given five words (ice cream, flower, President Ford, dog, atom), students can record other words in stream-of-consciousness fashion moving from the first word on to more abstract, emotive terms. Example: "dog, fuzzy, brown, warm, friendly, love," etc.

3. Given a list of ten randomly selected words from a dictionary, students rank order the words and their definitions, depending upon the presence of words with clear referents in the definition. For example, the definition of "cat" contains numerous nouns while the definition of "with" does not.

4. An extension of number three above asks students to create a class dictionary for words used in a current fad among young people. Again, the definitions would be analyzed for the presence or absence of clear referents.

5. Having listened to three songs—a folk ballad, a nursery rhyme, and an instrumental, students could discuss the correlation between the clarity or simplicity of the meaning and the presence or ambiguity of referents for each song.

6. Students of formal grammar can list nonsense "words" in each form class—noun, verb, adjective, adverb, and function word. Then the "words" could be placed under two categories labeled "words with clear referents" and "words with ambiguous or no referents."

7. Given one descriptive paragraph and a transitional, introductory, or summary paragraph, students who tabulated the number of words with clear referents in each paragraph begin to understand both the referential function of words and some reasons for the use of both concrete and abstract words.

8. To see correlations between the presence of clear referents and the clarity of meaning, students can construct abstraction ladders such as the following:

human being
man
athlete
football player
quarterback
Pat Sullivan

9. Pose the following situation and issue for class discussion.[1] A youngster chases a squirrel to a tree; and as often happens, the squirrel keeps the tree between itself and the youngster as he runs round and round the tree trying to get a good look at the squirrel. Did the youngster ever go around the squirrel? (Some will suppose "go around" refers to the act of passing the squirrel as when one car passes another. Other students might believe that once the youngster has circled the tree he has gone around the squirrel, regardless of what the squirrel does.) The point is that words with ambiguous meanings often have more than one plausible referent.

10. Ask students if the following sentences have meaning. Why? Why not?

a) The present king of France is bald.

b) It was a round square.

Individually or in groups, students who identify referents for words by placing them in groups according to the presence of a clear referent understand that while some words have referents others may not. Other exercises above expand the students' ability to handle the referential principle in a functional way. These exercises help explain why some semanticists and many readers criticize the use of vague and abstract language. These exercises also suggest the care with which teachers should advise students to use concrete words—words whose referents are clear.

Even when referents are identifiable, as in the case of proper nouns and class nouns naming physical objects, problems with referents spring up in a new form. Whereas it is obvious that the referent of a word must be something the five senses can perceive in some way or another, it is not obvious *what* the senses are to perceive. When a set of eyes looks at a cup, what is seen? The cup? Or do eyes see only a portion of the cup, say a part of the outer surface of the cup? The referent for the word "cup" could be the whole cup, but it could also be the perceiver's visual image

---

[1]Edward R. Levy and Charlene H. Tibbetts, *Rhetoric in Thought and Writing* (New York: Holt, Rinehart and Winston, 1972), bk. 2, p. 3.

(sense-datum) of a relatively small part of the cup.[2] Language based exercises focused on the referents of words can lead students to an understanding of the tenuous hold words have on reality, to in-depth understanding of levels of abstraction in language, and to first impressions of the correlation between perceiving and writing. The following exercises stimulate curiosity and help students understand two ways of seeing something so ordinary as a cup or so mystical as the printed page.

1. Given either an ink blot or a spontaneous design drawn on the board, students can differentiate between two kinds of referents and two kinds of seeing—those low in abstraction and those high in abstraction. Once the ink blot is projected on a screen or once a spontaneous design is drawn on the board, students can be asked the question, "What do you see?" In the host of varied answers, some students will give answers similar to one of the following: "I see a dark colored splotch" or "I see a bunch of yellow lines on a green board." Once answers are given which do not give a name to or imply that there is an object in the ink blot or in the spontaneous design, this exercise is completed. Students ought to know what it means to look only at the visual image before them—an image of little meaning and one very low in abstraction.

2. Hold a multicolored cup up for all to see, and ask, "What do you see in my hand?"

Answer: "A cup."

Answer: "A cylindrical, multicolored shape about four inches high and about three inches wide with a bump on one side."

Answers of the second kind suggest preception at low levels of abstraction—the level at which the referent for the word "cup is a mere sense-datum.

3. Asking the following questions helps some students differentiate between low-level abstractions and high-level abstractions as referents for words.

[2]The semantic point here is that under the limits of human perception and language, the referent and meaning of even such a clear word as "cup" may not be a solid, simple object but rather something so vague and private as a personal, visual image. This private visual image is known as a sense-datum, and sense-data could be introduced as possible referents and meanings of words.

What is it that a hunter sees when he mistakes a peculiar combination of colors, shapes, and movement in the woods for the front half of a deer?

What is it that is seen when an object such as an unusually large dog is so far off that it is visible but not recognizeable?

What does a child see when he or she calls a cow a big dog?

What is it that is seen when a viewer looks first at a ship far out to sea and then at the same ship next to the dock?

4. What does each person see when one person looks at this picture

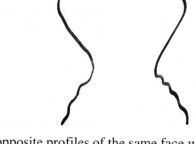

and sees opposite profiles of the same face while the other person sees a vase? Some teachers may want to lead from a discussion about the face-vase picture to a general discussion about why people disagree on the meanings of words, about what makes reading a difficult task unless the reader "sees the words in the right way," or about right and wrong interpretations of literature.

5. If students are asked to read and write concrete poetry, they are encouraged to pay special attention to the visual image of the poem—a kind of seeing which is low in abstraction. Once poems have been written or collected, the teacher of semantics can ask students what they·see. Appropriate for readers of concrete poetry, this question leads toward answers which are low in abstraction such as "words in the shape of a worm," "words in the shape of a stamped envelope" and so on depending on the poem.

6. To encourage the recognition and use of words low in abstraction—words whose referents are relatively clear—the teacher can ask students to write descriptive paragraphs in which many words appeal to one or more of the five senses.

7. In contrast to the writing in exercise 6 above, students can write definitions for the words "ego," "honesty," "charisma," "transportation," or "understanding." The presence or absence of identifiable referents should be discussed in descriptive writing on one hand and in writing of definitions on the other.

8. Another way to explain the difference between two ways of seeing is to introduce the concepts of *sensory perception* and *reasoned content*. Using a collection of pictures, the teacher of semantics asks what students see without using their powers of reason or imagination. Most likely students' answers will be responses of sensory perception and will be stated in words whose referents are clear. A second kind of question about the pictures ("What does this picture mean?") will stimulate answers involving reason, imagination, and words without clear referents.

Students will rightfully question the significance of the above exercises. Looking at cups, inkblots, and pictures in a search for referents and in search of differences between low- and high-level abstraction seems a long way from learning to use words effectively. Depending upon the grade level, the students, and the teacher, the study of words' referents and the search for referents can be done quickly and painlessly, for students need to understand only two basic ideas: 1) that words carry meaning to the degree they unambiguously serve a referential function and 2) that the difficulty semanticists have identifying unambiguous referents parallels and partially explains the difficulty speakers and writers have giving clear meaning to words, sentences, paragraphs, and ideas. In some classrooms the activities suggested above will need supplementary discussion in addition to alteration; in other classrooms, the activities suggested above may be sufficient or even repetitious. Whatever the case, students should realize that everyone should expect difficulties when he or she attempts to make a word's meaning universally clear.

Difficulty identifying referents for words has its parallel in the difficulty students face when they fail to write concretely maintaining touch with reality; therefore, semantic principles should appear indirectly and implicitly in the teaching of composition.

Students ought to realize that, like a word, a sentence without clear referents is meaningless; that to make meanings clear, writers use very concrete sentences; and that paragraphs contain linguistic movements up and down ladders of abstraction. It is not that all abstractions are bad or that concrete sentences are always good: the point is that the reader must be able to follow the writer up and down ladders of abstraction as represented by topic sentences, sentences containing facts, exemplifying sentences, concluding sentences, and so on. Whereas the previous suggested activities focus directly upon the study of semantics, the semantic questions and language exercises below indirectly and implicitly engage students in the study of semantics as they write and as they study composition.

Whether they are called topic sentences, controlling sentences, main sentences, main ideas, or top sentences, certain sentences in many paragraphs stand out as ones encompassing a paragraph's major point of view. These sentences tend to be the most abstract—often so abstract as to give only glimpses of meaning. Often other slightly less abstract, *clarifying sentences* offer definitions, restatements, or narrowed interpretations of the key idea in the *topic sentence*. Sentences providing examples, statistics, facts, analogies, testimony, and other supporting information reach even lower levels of abstraction. Finally, in the deductive paragraph, the *concluding sentence* returns to the highest levels of abstraction along with the topic sentence. *Although they have a way of not fitting simplistic models such as this one*, paragraphs include movements up and down ladders of abstraction; and students who wander from their topics, grope vaguely around topics, or indulge in cliché profit from explanations and exercises concerning the semantic functions of concrete and abstract words and sentences. In hypothetical, deductive paragraphs, both the writer and the reader start off with a highly abstract topic sentence, move down just a bit to a slightly lower level of abstraction in a clarifying sentence, drop rapidly in abstraction to sentences of examples and details, and at the end move back to the high level of abstraction in the first sentence, the topic sentence.

While models and formulas serve as illustrations of linguistic acts appearing in pieces of writing, they are relatively useless in teaching the composing process. Formulas and models can, however, be used both safely and effectively to explain semantic principles at the sentence and paragraph levels. Students who have applied the concept of the abstraction ladder to paragraphs and to sentences of their own understand why vagueness, ambiguity, and cliché characterize writers who fail to use examples, facts, analogies, and other ways of making meaning clear. Students can understand why teachers of writing like to talk about topic sentences, why they criticize jargon, and why they search for detail in writing. Such understanding might not tell students *how to write*, but it will help them understand language, its use in writing, and the close relationship between thinking and writing. The following exercises have been selected as examples of ways to teach semantic principles implicitly in the teaching of writing.

1. Provided the following formulas, students can complete exercises related to the study of semantics and writing.[3]

$$P = TS + CS + D_1 + D_2 + D_3 + D_4 + SS$$
$$P = D_1 + D_2 + D_3 + D_4 + CS + TS$$

Given sentence *a* below as a topic sentence and the other sentences in random order, students list the other sentences in order of decreasing abstraction.

a) Cars cause problems because cars take so much space.

e) The Springfield City Council spent three hours last Friday night deciding whether or not to allow Penny's to add five floors to its downtown building.

b) Decatur paid a consulting firm twenty-five thousand dollars to study the effects of allowing a new shopping center to locate on the west end of Decatur.

d) One-half of the downtown area is taken up by streets, parking lots, and service stations.

---

[3]When P means paragraph, TS means topic sentence, CS means clarifying sentence, D means detail, and SS means summary sentence, these formulas represent model deductive and inductive paragraphs.

c) Mr. Jones, who is on the city council, quit because the mayor would not agree to build bike paths.

f) (One car takes up over one hundred square feet—enough space for a small tree or tulip bed.)

2. Using the sentences above, identify the most concrete sentences by the number of concrete words whose referents are clear. (Complete consensus will be impossible to achieve.) Some teachers may want to compare the number of words whose referents seem to be physical objects, mental objects, or sense data.

3. Suppose that the proper ratio of concrete and abstract sentences were six to one. Strictly for purposes of explanation and practice, students would write paragraphs containing six concrete sentences for every abstract one.

4. Students can experiment with the referential principle by composing short descriptive essays or "poems" in which topics or objects of study are discussed using words according to one or more of the following rules:

a) Three-fourths of the words' referents must be physical objects.

b) No word can have an apparent physical object as its referent.

c) Half of the words must be words identifying sense-data.

d) All words must have only sense-data as their referents.

These unusual rules demand patience, but they give students an understanding of the effects of using words representing different levels of abstraction.

5. The biases of concrete terminology and differences in points of view are exposed when students are given a common topic, "student rights" for example, and asked to participate in two writing exercises. One group of students is asked to narrow the topic and treat it as "scientifically" as possible emphasizing facts and very guarded and unpretentious generalizations. This group of students would be encouraged to use many words whose referents were obvious. A second group of students would be asked to write a polemic on the same topic. Although students' thoughts expressed in this assignment are more important, the teacher might point out the levels of abstraction in each group's writing.

The most important reward to be gained from the study of

semantics is an understanding of reasons to be skeptical of the ability of words to reflect reality. While students know that not all words in print tell ultimate truths, while students know writing clearly is difficult, and while students know abstract words are hard to understand, students too often do not understand why words so apparently simple individually can be so unbelievably difficult to handle collectively. Students of English who study semantics and who learn about composition through a semantic perspective might very well appreciate an understanding of semantics.

Index

Abstract. *See* Semantic

Adjective: inflections, 32; inflectional loss in ME (Middle English), 35; forms in social dialects, 88; structural analysis of, 102

Adjunctive: genitival, 6

Adolescent: view of reality, 7–9

Adverb: flat, 32–33; function of prepositional phrases, 99; structural analysis of, 102

Affixation: in nouns, 5; in irregular nominals, 14; word formation through, 17

Africanism: as a cultural force in dialects, 81; pidginized forms of Americanisms, 90

All, 86

Alphabet: changes in English graphemes, 31–33; development of 44–45

American: and British English, 14; regionalisms, 15–16; ethnic literature, 20; dictionaries, 50; English usage, 66; dialects, 80–95; and Canadian dialects, 82; "general," 86; Negro dialects, 90

American College Dictionary, 52

American Heritage Dictionary, 52

Analytic: character of English language, 31

Angleworm, 86

Anglo-Saxon: sources of Old English (OE), 31–33; ninth-century communities, 33; *Chronicle*, 33; Norman-French influences on, 33–34

Aspect: classical treatment of, 5; transformational view of, 103

Awl, 86

Bag, 86

Bailey, Nathaniel: early eighteenth-century dictionaries of, 49

Balto-Slavic: languages, 27

Base component: transformational concern with, 104–5

Baugh, Albert C., 29, 34

Behavioral. *See* Verbal

Black dialects: provinciality toward, 80; Africanisms and, 81; and geographic mobility, 86; myths about, 89; origins of, 89–90; characteristics of, 90–91

Blinds, 86

Blount, Thomas: glossary of neologisms and foreign expressions, 49

Borrowings: as a part of language pedagogy, 11; as major vocabulary source, 19–20; from Romance languages, 26

Bout, 86

Braddock, Lloyd-Jones, and Schoer: *Research in the Teaching of English Composition*, 97

British: and American English, 14; colonial expansion, 26; dialects, 81

Bucket, 86

Can't, 86

Carry, 86

Case: in classical vs. schoolroom grammars, 5; genitives, 5–6; inflectional loss to signal, 31–33; genitives in black English, 91

Celtic: influence on Old English (OE), 33, origins of OE place-names, 34

Century Dictionary, 51

English Sentences, 101
Escort, 86
Ethnic: dialects, 80–81
Etymology: exercises in, 14; as index to history and heritage, 19; apparent inconsistencies in, 32; dictionaries of, 49; reputable dictionaries of, 51; exercises, 57; historical tracings, 59; fallacy, 61; denotation and connotation in, 62; semantic changes, 63; elevation and degradation in, 64–65
Euphemisms: adolescent disdain for, 8; in dictionary exercises, 61–63
Evestrough, 86
Extraposition: transformational concern with, 103

Farley, F. E.: Advanced English Grammar, 97
Features: lexical, grammatical, distinctive, 105
Ferry, 86
Florida FL Reporter, 90
Fog, 86
Formal: usage levels, 68–69; grammar study as influence on verbal skills, 97; usage change in traditionalist view, 99; criteria for traditional classification of parts of speech, 100
Fountain, 86
French: influence on Old English (OE), 32; sources of Old-Middle English (ME) words, 34; ecclesiastical, social, political, military, legal, medical lexical sources in ME, 36; dialects of, 81
Frying pan, 86
Function: in nouns, 5; linguistic, 11; of formal grammar study, 97; as basis for traditional classification of parts of speech, 100
Funk, Isaac Kaufman: lexicographical contributions of, 51

Gender: "natural" in Modern English (MnE), 35
"General American" dialect, 86
Generative. See Transformationalist
Genitive. See Case
Germanic: languages, 27; low and high, 27; cognates, 31
Goober, 86
Gove, Phillip: ed., W-3, 55–56
Grammar: "schoolroom," 3; drills, 3; as verbal etiquette, 4; prescriptive, 4; classical, 5; schoolroom vs. classical, 5–6;

tense and aspect in, 5; case in, 5; descriptive and prescriptive, 5; systems that "leak," 6; pedagogy and, 10; as a part of the overall plan for language study, 13; induction in teaching of, 17; and composition, 22; dialectal peculiarities of, 81; of black dialects, 90; basic principles, 96–98; lay definition of, 96; and dialectal peculiarities, 97; and writing skills, 97; pedagogy, 98; traditional, 98–100; structural, 100–102; transformational, 102–5
Grease, 86
Greasy, 86
Great Vowel Shift: influence on spelling and pronunciation, 32; sixteenth- and seventeenth-century changes from, 37; theories of causes for, 37–38
Grimm, Jacob, 29
Gullah: dialect, 90
Gutter, 86

Hellenic: languages, 27; influences on traditionalism, 99
History: of English conventions, 11; as a part of overall language plan, 13; of British and American English, 13; reflected in international borrowings, 19–20; of British-American English, 25–47; of prestigious English dialects, 81; as a political and cultural force on dialects, 81–82; and migratory influences, 83, 86; and classical influences on traditionalism, 99
Hog, 86
Holmes, Stewart W.: Meaning in Language, 8
Hook and Matthews: See Modern American Grammar and Usage
House, 86

Idiolect: defined, 81; exercise in, 92–94
Independent clause, 100
Indo-European: Proto, 27; language family chart, 28
Indo-Iranian: languages, 27
Inflection: genitival, 5; simplification of, 26–27; loss, 31; genitive and plural, 32; adverbial and adjectival, 32; nominals in Modern English (MnE), 35; in social dialects, 87–88; in black English, 91

Jargon: teen-age, 2
Jespersen, Otto, 5

Johnson, Samuel: nineteenth-century lexicographical work of, 50
Jonson, Ben, 49–50

Kenyon, John: on "cultural levels and functional varieties," 68–69
Kersey, John: eighteenth-century dictionary of, 49
Kittredge, George: *Advanced English Grammar*, 97
Krapp, George Philip, 68
Kurath, Hans. *See Linguistic Atlas of the United States and Canada*

Language: humane values in, 3–4; defined, 4; traditional classroom experiences in, 4; student-centered, 4; influences on change in, 4–5; flux or change in, 6; as an index to reality, 7–8; dialects and diversity, 11; history of English, 11; borrowings, 11; logic in, 17; as a social tool, 18; of lower animals, 19; cultural influences on, 19; and literature, 20; emotion in, 21; and literary history, 21; and composition, 21; accuracy and precision in writing, 22; Teutonic, 26; in *W-3* controversy, 55–56; varieties of usage, 67; in context, 74; based provinciality, 80; traditional view of, 98–100; structural view of, 100–102; transformational view of, 102–5; acquisition, 104
Language and Mind, 104
Latin: cognates in English, 31; influences on Old English (OE), 33; invasion and influence on OE home terms, place-names, political terms, 34; paradigmatic model of traditionalists, 99
Law and order, 86
Lester, Mark: *See Readings in Applied Transformational Grammar*
Lexical: vs. grammatical meaning, 5; change, 11; variety, 26; sources in Old-Middle English, 34; and phonological peculiarities in North, South, Midland areas, 86
Lexicalist: contrast between transformationalist and, 103
Lexicography: survey of, pedagogy and, 11; as part of the overall language plan, 13; use of dictionary, 14; student exercises in, 16; as an index to heritage and history, 19; historical backgrounds of, 48–51; principles of, 51–55; controversies in, 55–56; exercises in, 57; class-

room exercises in, 57–65; usage varieties in, 71
Lexicon: influences on, 4–5; borrowings, 11, slang, 16; sources of and patterns in, 17–18; in English from Germanic sources, 29; dialectal variations in, 81; pedagogy and regional, 81; exercises in dialectal, 92
Liebert, Burt. *See Linguistics and the New English Teacher*
Linguistic: myths about black English, 89
Linguistic Atlas of the United States and Canada, 82
Linguistics and the New English Teacher, 101
Linking verb; structural analysis of, 102
L-lessness: in black English, 90
London: historically prestigious dialect of, 81

McDavid, Ravin I., Jr.: *Linguistic Atlas of the United States and Canada*, 82; on social dialects, 87–88
Marry, 86
Mary, 86
Meaning: lexical vs. grammatical, 5; etymological exercises, 14; ambiguity in, 16; in dictionary study, 49–51; denotative and connotative, 62; shifts in, 63–65; as basis for traditional classifications of parts of speech, 100; transformationalist concern with, 103; and composition, 121
Mental discipline: approach to language pedagogy, 6; and paradigmatic memorization, 96–97
Merriam-Webster Third New International Dictionary (W-3): controversy over, 55; mentioned, 53
Merry, 86
Middle English (ME): phonological changes in, 32; French influences on, 32; double negative in, 33; political influences on, 34; major linguistic changes in, 35
Midland: dialectal region, 82
Mind: transformational concern with, 103
Minsheu: publication of *Ductor in Linguas*, 49
Modern American Grammar and Usage, 101
Monroe, Walter S. *See Encyclopedia of Educational Research*
Morph. *See* Morphology; Structuralist
Morpheme. *See* Morphology; Structuralist

Morphology: of nouns, 5; lexical vs. grammatical meaning, 5; exercises in irregular nominal plurals, 14; vocabulary building through, 17; sources in Old-Middle English, 34; in black English, 91; as traditional criteria for classifying parts of speech, 100; as subsystem of grammar, 100; as empirical evidence, 101

Mrs., 86

Natural language: grammatical systems in, 97

Negative: double, 33; multiples for intensification, 33; avoidance of double, 72

Neologisms: sources to explore, 16; resisted by formal language, 98

New England: dialects on TV, 80; dialectal prestige of, 81; *Linguistic Atlas* delineation of, 82

Nominal: subject, 100; object, 100

Nonstandard: usage, 66; criteria and principles of, 67–77; pedagogic attitudes toward, 82

Norman: Conquest, 33; French influences on Middle English, 33–34

North: and North-Midland dialectal regions, 82; geographic identification of, 83; dialectal characteristics of, 86

North: dialectal region, 82

Northern Inland: dialectal predominance of, 80

Noun: and noun phrase traditionally defined, 99; structural analysis of, 101–2

Oil, 86

Old English: characteristics of, 31–33; influences on lexicon of, 34

Old Norse: influences on Old English (OE), 33; influences on ME lexicon, 34

Onomastics: exercises in, 15, 95

Oral. *See* Speech

Orange, 86

Orthography: changes in English, 31–32; sixteenth- and seventeenth-century standardization in, 37

Orwell, George, 21

Out, 86

Oxford English Dictionary (OED): early editions, 49; Murray's editorship of, 50; Craigie's American English edition of, 51; superiority of, 53

Pail, 86

Paradigm: memorizations of, 96; model of traditionalism, 99

Paragraph construct, 122–23

Paris: historically prestigious dialect of, 81

Parts of speech: traditionally defined, 100; transformationally defined, 105

Passivization: transformational concern with, 103

Patterns of English, 101

PDAE. *See* Present Day American English

Peanut, 86

Pedagogy: general, 10; spontaneity and, 12; need for overall plan, 12; sequencing language experiences, 12; six aspects of the overall language plan, 13; practical exercises, 13–14; spontaneity for language, 14; motivation and, 14; variety as a part of planning, 15; onomastics, 15; usage, 15–16; inductive, 17; relating language and literature, 20; relation language and composition, 21–23; teacher competence and effective language, 23–24; lexicography and, 54–55; and principles of usage, 66–77; for combating dialectal prejudices, 80; and nonstandard or regional speech, 82; and grammar, 98; second language, 101

Perfect(ive). *See* Aspect

Performance: transformational concern with, 104–5

Periphrastic: genitival, 6

Phillips, Edward: *New World of Words* (1678), 49

Philology: nineteenth-century, 29; Minsheu's contributions to, 49

Phone. *See* Phonology; Structuralist

Phonology: English correlations and sound shifts, 29; changes in English, 31–33; signals in dictionaries, 51, 55; dialectal, 81; regional peculiarities of, 86; peculiarities of social, 87; in black English, 91; exercises in dialectal, 94; as a part of grammars, 97; as subsystem of grammar, 100; as empirical evidence, 101; transformational concern with, 103–4

Phrase: traditional classification of, 99; structural analysis of, 101–2

Phrase structure rules: in structuralist syntax, 100–102; in transformational syntax, 104

Index   133